STRATEGIC INFORMATION WARFARE

A New Face of War

Roger C. Molander/Andrew S. Riddile/Peter A. Wilson

Prepared for the
Office of the Secretary of Defense

National Defense Research Institute

RAND

This report summarizes research performed by RAND for the Office of the Assistant Secretary of Defense (Command, Control, Communications and Intelligence). The objective of this effort was to garner perspectives on a broad range of potential national security issues related to the evolving concept of information warfare, with a particular emphasis on the defensive aspects of what is characterized in the report as "strategic information warfare." The study was undertaken in recognition that future U.S. national security strategy is likely to be profoundly affected by the ongoing rapid evolution of cyberspace—the global information infrastructure—and in this context by the growing dependence of the U.S. military and other national institutions and infrastructures on potentially vulnerable elements of the U.S. national information infrastructure.

This report should be of special interest to those who are exploring the effect of the information revolution on warfare. It should also be of interest to those segments of the U.S. and broader international security community that are concerned with the post–cold war evolution of military and national security strategy, especially strategy changes driven wholly or in part by the evolution of, and possible revolutions in, technology.

The research reported here was accomplished within the Acquisition and Technology Policy Center of RAND's National Defense Research Institute, a federally funded research and development center sponsored by the Office of the Secretary of Defense, the Joint Staff, and the defense agencies. It builds on an earlier and ongoing body of research within that center on the national security implications of the information revolution.

CONTENTS

FIGURES

TABLES

> We live in an age that is driven by information. Technological breakthroughs . . .
> are *changing the face of war* and how we prepare for war.
>
> —William Perry, Secretary of Defense

INFORMATION WARFARE AND THE CHANGING FACE OF WAR

Information warfare (IW) represents a rapidly evolving and, as yet, imprecisely defined field of growing interest for defense planners and policymakers. The source of both the interest and the imprecision in this field is the so-called information revolution—led by the ongoing rapid evolution of cyberspace, microcomputers, and associated information technologies. The U.S. defense establishment, like U.S. society as a whole, is moving rapidly to take advantage of the new opportunities presented by these changes. At the same time, current and potential U.S. adversaries (and allies) are also looking to exploit the evolving global information infrastructure and associated technologies for military purposes.

The end result and implications of these ongoing changes for international and other forms of conflict are highly uncertain, befitting a subject that is this new and dynamic. Will IW be a new but subordinate facet of warfare in which the United States and its allies readily overcome their own potential cyberspace vulnerabilities and gain and sustain whatever tactical and strategic military advantages that might be available in this arena? Or will the changes in conflict wrought by the ongoing information revolution be so rapid and profound that the net result is a new and grave threat to traditional military operations and U.S. society that fundamentally changes the future character of warfare?

In response to this situation and these uncertainties, in January 1995 the Secretary of Defense formed the IW Executive Board to facilitate "the development and achievement of national information warfare goals." In support of this effort, RAND was asked to provide and exercise an analytic framework for identifying key IW issues, exploring their consequences and highlighting starting points for IW-related policy development—looking to help develop a sustainable national consensus on an overall U.S. IW strategy.

To accomplish this purpose, RAND conducted an exercise-based framing and analysis of what we came to call the "strategic information warfare" problem. Involving senior members of the national security community as well as representatives from national security-related telecommunications and information systems industries, the exercises led participants through a challenging hypothetical IW crisis involving a major regional political-military contingency. The exercise methodology, known by the label "The Day After . . . ," had been previously used for a variety of nuclear proliferation, counterproliferation, and related intelligence studies. The specific scenario chosen for the exercise involved a turn-of-the-century conflict between Iran and the United States and its allies, focused on a threat to Saudi Arabia.

The exercise was conducted six times in evolving versions over the course of five months from January to June 1995. Each iteration allowed for refinement of basic strategic IW concepts and provided further insights about their national security implications. This process provided an opportunity to assess and analyze the perspectives of senior participants from government and industry regarding such matters as the plausibility of strategic IW scenarios such as the one presented, possible evolutions in related threats and vulnerabilities, and the phrasing of key associated strategy and policy issues. It also provided an opportunity to identify emerging schools of thought and, in some cases, a rough consensus on next steps on a number of important strategic IW issues.

In addition, the process yielded a badly needed multidimensional framework for sharpening near-term executive branch focus on the development of strategic IW policy, strategy, and goals—in particular regarding the implications of prospective major regional contingencies on defensive IW strategies, doctrines, vulnerabilities, and capabilities. It also provided a highly useful forum for beginning to coordinate with industry on the future direction of IW-related national security telecommunications strategy.

As can be inferred from the above comments, the methodology employed in this study appears to offer particular advantages for addressing many of the conceptual difficulties inherent in this topic. The subject matter is very new and, in some dimensions, technically complex, especially for individuals typically found in policy-making positions. The challenge of finding techniques for efficiently accelerating the process of basic education on the topic and its implications for national security policy and strategy cannot be underestimated.

This report presents the results of this study. Specifically, the purpose of this report is to

- describe and frame the concept of strategic information warfare

- describe and discuss the key features and related issues that characterize strategic IW

- explore the consequences of these features and issues for U.S. national security as illuminated by the exercises

- suggest analytical and policy directions for addressing elements of these strategic IW features and issues.

STRATEGIC INFORMATION WARFARE

The United States has substantial information-based resources, including complex management systems and infrastructures involving the control of electric power, money flow, air traffic, oil and gas, and other information-dependent items. U.S. allies and potential coalition partners are similarly increasingly dependent on various information infrastructures. Conceptually, if and when potential adversaries attempt to damage these systems using IW techniques, information warfare inevitably takes on a strategic aspect.

Strategic Information Warfare and Post–Cold War Strategy

Our exercise scenario highlighted from the start a fundamental aspect of strategic information warfare: There is no "front line." Strategic targets in the United States may be just as vulnerable to attack as in-theater command, control, communications, and intelligence (C3I) targets. As a result, the attention of exercise participants quickly broadened beyond a single traditional regional theater of operations to *four* distinct separate theaters of operation as portrayed in Figure S.1: the battlefield per se; allied "Zones of Interior" (in our scenario, the sovereign territory of Saudi Arabia); the intercontinental zone of communication and deployment; and the U.S. Zone of Interior.

The post–cold war "over there" focus of the regional component of U.S. national military strategy is therefore rendered incomplete for this kind of scenario and is of declining relevance to the likely future international strategic environment. When responding to information warfare attacks of this character, military strategy can no longer afford to focus on conducting and supporting operations only in the region of concern. An in-depth examination of the implications of IW for the U.S. and allied infrastructures that depend on the unimpeded management of information is also required.

RAND *MR661-S.1*

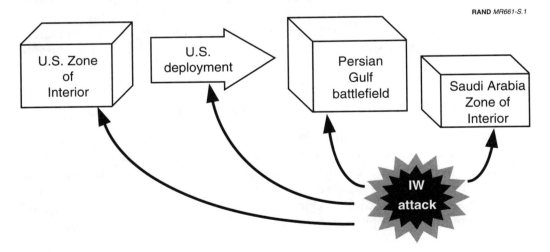

Figure S.1—The Changing Face of War: Four Strategic IW Theaters of Operation

The Basic Features of Strategic Information Warfare

The exercises highlighted seven defining features of strategic information warfare:

- *Low entry cost:* Unlike traditional weapon technologies, development of information-based techniques does not require sizable financial resources or state sponsorship. Information systems expertise and access to important networks may be the only prerequisites.

- *Blurred traditional boundaries:* Traditional distinctions—public versus private interests, warlike versus criminal behavior—and geographic boundaries, such as those between nations as historically defined, are complicated by the growing interaction within the information infrastructure.

- *Expanded role for perception management:* New information-based techniques may substantially increase the power of deception and of image-manipulation activities, dramatically complicating government efforts to build political support for security-related initiatives.

- *A new strategic intelligence challenge:* Poorly understood strategic IW vulnerabilities and targets diminish the effectiveness of classical intelligence collection and analysis methods. A new field of analysis focused on strategic IW may have to be developed.

- *Formidable tactical warning and attack assessment problems:* There is currently no adequate tactical warning system for distinguishing between strategic IW attacks and other kinds of cyberspace activities, including espionage or accidents.

- *Difficulty of building and sustaining coalitions:* Reliance on coalitions is likely to increase the vulnerabilities of the security postures of all the partners to strategic IW attacks, giving opponents a disproportionate strategic advantage.

- *Vulnerability of the U.S. homeland:* Information-based techniques render geographical distance irrelevant; targets in the continental United States are just as vulnerable as in-theater targets. Given the increased reliance of the U.S. economy and society on a high-performance networked information infrastructure, a new set of lucrative strategic targets presents itself to potential IW-armed opponents.

CONSEQUENCES OF THE BASIC FEATURES

Through the course of our exercise-based analysis, we prompted policymakers and other experts from the public and private sectors to explore the character and consequences of these features. The discussion that follows summarizes our synthesis of observations made by the exercise participants on the characteristics and implications of these features for the strategic IW problem. Note that there is a "cascading" effect inherent in these observations—each helps to create the enabling conditions for subsequent ones.

Low Entry Cost

Interconnected networks may be subject to attack and disruption not just by states but also by nonstate actors, including dispersed groups and even individuals. Potential adversaries could also possess a wide range of capabilities. Thus, the threat to U.S. interests could be multiplied substantially and will continue to change as ever more complex systems are developed and the requisite expertise is ever more widely diffused.

Some participants believed that the entry price to many of the IW attack options posited could be raised by denying easy access to networks and control systems through the exploitation of new software encryption techniques. Other participants acknowledged that this might mitigate some threats but emphasized that this approach would not remove other threats to an internetted system by a corrupted insider (systems operator) and/or direct physical attack. It would also increase the difficulty in strategic and tactical intelligence vis-a-vis strategic IW attackers.

Blurred Traditional Boundaries

Given the wide array of possible opponents, weapons, and strategies, it becomes increasingly difficult to distinguish between foreign and domestic sources of IW threats and actions. You may not know who's under attack by whom, or who's in charge of the attack. This greatly complicates the traditional role distinction between domestic law enforcement, on the one hand, and national security and intelligence entities, on the other. Another consequence of this blurring phenomenon is the disappearance of clear distinctions between different levels of anti-state activity, ranging from crime to warfare. Given this blurring, nation-states opposed to U.S. strategic interests could forgo more traditional types of military or terrorist action and instead exploit individuals or transnational criminal organizations (TCOs) to conduct "strategic criminal operations."

Expanded Role for Perception Management

Opportunities for IW agents to manipulate information that is key to public perceptions may increase. For example, political action groups and other nongovernment organizations can utilize the Internet to galvanize political support, as the Zapitistas in Chiapas, Mexico, were able to do. Furthermore, the possibility arises that the very "facts" of an event can be manipulated via multimedia techniques and widely disseminated. Conversely, there may be a decreased capability to build and maintain domestic support for controversial political actions. One implication is that future U.S. administrations may include a robust Internet component as part of any public information campaign.

Among participants, there was no support for any extraordinary maneuver by the government to "seize control" of the media and the Internet in response to a probable IW attack. Rather, there was an acknowledgment that future U.S. administrations might face a daunting task in shaping and sustaining domestic support for any action marked by a high degree of ambiguity and uncertainty in the IW realm.

Lack of Strategic Intelligence

For a variety of reasons, traditional intelligence-gathering and analysis methods may be of limited use in meeting the strategic IW intelligence challenge. Collection targets are difficult to identify; allocation of intelligence resources is difficult because of the rapidly changing nature of the threat; and vulnerabilities and target sets are not, as yet, well understood. In sum, the United States may have difficulty identifying potential adversaries, their intentions, and their capabilities. One implication of this is that new organizational relationships are needed within the intelligence community and between this community and other entities. A restructuring of roles and missions may also be required.

In our exercises, debate on this problem centered on the need for some interagency structure to allow for coordinated collection and analysis of "foreign" and "domestic" sources versus the desire to preserve the boundary between foreign intelligence and domestic law enforcement.

Difficulty of Tactical Warning and Attack Assessment

This feature of warfare presents fundamentally new problems in a cyberspace environment. A basic problem is distinguishing between "attacks" and other events, such as accidents, system failures, or hacking by "thrill-seekers." The main consequence of this feature is that the United States may not know when an attack is under way, who is attacking, or how the attack is being conducted.

As in the debate over what to do about the dilemmas posed by the strategic intelligence challenge, exercise participants split on this topic between those who were prepared to consider a more radical mixing of domestic law enforcement and foreign intelligence institutions and those strongly opposed to any commingling.

Difficulty of Building and Sustaining Coalitions

Many U.S. allies and coalition partners will be vulnerable to IW attacks on their core information infrastructures. For example, the dependence on cellular phones in developing countries could well render telephone communications in those nations highly susceptible to disruption. Other sectors in the early stages of exploiting the information revolution (e.g., energy and financial) may also present vulnerabilities that an adversary might attack to undermine coalition participation. Such attacks might also serve to sever "weak links" in the execution of coalition plans. Conversely, tentative coalition partners who urgently need military assistance may want assurances that a U.S. deployment plan to their region is not vulnerable to IW disruption.

There was general agreement among participants that as the United States develops and refines defensive systems and concepts of operations or techniques in this area, it should consider sharing them with key allies, but no specific policies were proffered in the discussions.

Vulnerability of the U.S. Homeland

Information warfare has no front line. Potential battlefields are anywhere networked systems allow access. Current trends suggest that the U.S. economy will increasingly rely on complex, interconnected network control systems for such necessities as oil and gas pipelines, electric grids, etc. The vulnerability of these systems is currently poorly understood. In addition, the means of deterrence and retaliation are uncertain and may rely on traditional military instruments in addition to IW threats. In sum, the U.S. homeland may no longer provide a sanctuary from outside attack.

There was a broad consensus among exercise participants that no dramatic measures such as shutting down an infrastructure would be effective as a defensive measure (and some skepticism as to whether such action would, in fact, be possible during a crisis). There appeared, however, a broad consensus in favor of exploring the concept of a "minimum essential information infrastructure" based on a series of federally sponsored incentives to ensure that the owners and operators had procedures to detect IW-type attacks and reconstitution measures that minimized the impact of any one network disruption—see the discussion below.

AN ELUSIVE BOTTOM LINE ON THE THREAT

Over the course of the exercise series, careful attention was given to the possible solidifying of a bottom line on the gravity of the cyberspace-based strategic IW threat. Many existing information systems do appear to be vulnerable to some level of disruption or misuse. At the same time, developments in cyberspace are so dynamic that existing vulnerabilities may well be ameliorated as part of the natural building of immunities to threats that accompany any such rapidly evolving entity. However, our dependence on cyberspace and information systems generally is also growing rapidly—raising unsettling questions as to whether the "immune system" process can "keep up" and thus prevent serious strategic vulnerabilities from emerging and being exploited.

We looked for, but did not find, any strong statistical consensus on just where people think we are now on the threat spectrum portrayed in Figure S.2, or where we might be heading. We did observe, however, that over the course of the exercise, the general perspective on the magnitude of the strategic IW problem almost invariably appeared to move downward along the graph of Figure S.2. This experience mirrored that of the authors—the more time spent on this subject, the more one saw tough problems lacking concrete solutions and, in some cases, lacking even good ideas about where to start.

CONCLUSIONS

The features and likely consequences of strategic information warfare point to a basic conclusion: Key national military strategy assumptions are obsolescent and inadequate for confronting the threat posed by strategic IW. Five major recommendations emerged from the exercises as starting points for addressing this shortcoming:

RAND *MR661-S.2*

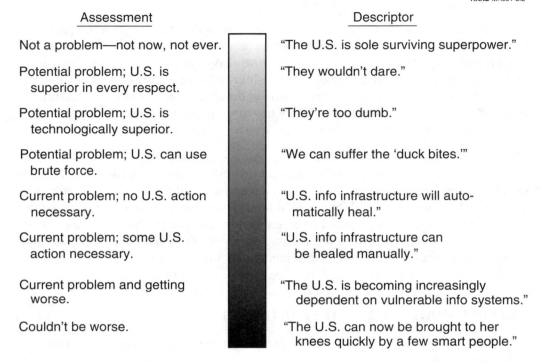

Assessment	Descriptor
Not a problem—not now, not ever.	"The U.S. is sole surviving superpower."
Potential problem; U.S. is superior in every respect.	"They wouldn't dare."
Potential problem; U.S. is technologically superior.	"They're too dumb."
Potential problem; U.S. can use brute force.	"We can suffer the 'duck bites.'"
Current problem; no U.S. action necessary.	"U.S. info infrastructure will automatically heal."
Current problem; some U.S. action necessary.	"U.S. info infrastructure can be healed manually."
Current problem and getting worse.	"The U.S. is becoming increasingly dependent on vulnerable info systems."
Couldn't be worse.	"The U.S. can now be brought to her knees quickly by a few smart people."

Figure S.2—A Broad Spectrum of Perspectives

1. Leadership: Who Should Be in Charge in the Government?

Participants widely agreed that an immediate and badly needed first step is the assignment of a focal point for federal government leadership in support of a coordinated U.S. response to the strategic IW threat. This focal point should be located in the Executive Office of the President, since only at this level can the necessary interagency coordination of the large number of government organizations involved in such matters—and the necessary interactions with the Congress—be effectively carried out. This office should also have the responsibility for close coordination with industry, since the nation's information infrastructure is being developed almost exclusively by the commercial sector. Once established, this high-level leadership should immediately take responsibility for initiating and managing a comprehensive review of national-level strategic information warfare issues.

2. Risk Assessment

The federal government leadership entity cited above should, as a first step, conduct an immediate risk assessment to determine, to the degree possible, the extent of the vulnerability of key elements of current U.S. national security and national military strategy to strategic information warfare. Strategic target sets, IW effects, and parallel vulnerability and threat assessments should be among the components of this review. In an environment of dynamic change in both cyberspace threats and vulnerabilities, there is no sound basis for presidential decisionmaking on strategic IW matters without such a risk assessment.

In this context there is always the hope or the belief—we saw both in the exercises—that the kind of aggressive response suggested in this report can be delayed while cyberspace gets a chance to evolve robust defenses on its own. This is, in fact, a possibility—that the healing and annealing of an immune system that is under constant assault, as cyberspace is and assuredly will continue to be (if only, in Willy Sutton's words, because that's where the money is), will create the robust national information infrastructure that everyone hopes to use. But it may not, and we are certainly not there now.

3. Government's Role

The appropriate role for government in responding to the strategic IW threat needs to be addressed, recognizing that this role—certain to be part leadership and part partnership with the domestic sector—will unquestionably evolve. In addition to being the performer of certain basic preparedness functions—such as organizing, equipping, training, and sustaining military forces—the government may play a more productive and efficient role as facilitator and maintainer of some information systems and infrastructure, and through policy mechanisms such as tax breaks to encourage reducing vulnerability and improving recovery and reconstitution capability.

An important factor is the traditional change in the government's role as one moves from national defense through public safety toward things that represent the public good. Clearly, the government's perceived role in this area will have to be balanced against public perceptions of the loss of civil liberties and the commercial sector's concern about unwarranted limits on its practices and markets.

4. National Security Strategy

Once an initial risk assessment has been completed, U.S. national security strategy needs to address preparedness for the threat as identified. As portrayed in Figure S.3, preparedness will cross several traditional boundaries from "military" to "civilian," from "foreign" to "domestic," and from "national" to "local."

One promising means for instituting this kind of preparedness could involve the concept of a "minimum essential information infrastructure" (MEII), which was introduced as a possible strategic defensive IW initiative in the exercise and is portrayed notionally in Figure S.3. The MEII is conceived as that minimum mixture of U.S. information systems, procedures, laws, and tax incentives necessary to ensure the nation's continued functioning even in the face of a sophisticated strategic IW attack. One facet of such an MEII might be a set of rules and regulations sponsored by the federal government to encourage the owners and operators of the various national infrastructures to take measures to reduce their infrastructure's vulnerability and/or to ensure rapid reconstitution in the face of IW-type attacks. The analog for

RAND *MR661-S.3*

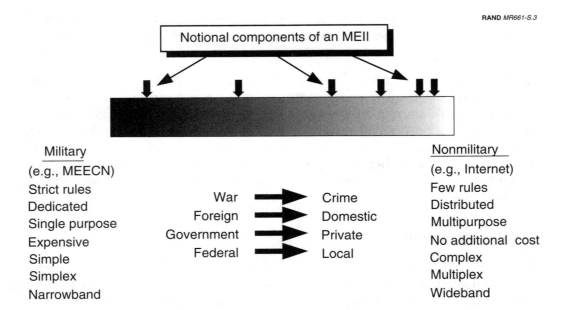

Figure S.3—A Spectrum of National Security Preparedness

this concept is the strategic nuclear Minimum Essential Emergency Communications Network (MEECN). Participants in the exercise found the MEII construct conceptually very attractive even though there was some uncertainty as to how it might be achieved. An assessment of the feasibility of an MEII (or like concepts) should be undertaken at an early date.

5. National Military Strategy

The current national military strategy emphasizes maintaining U.S. capability to project power into theaters of operation in key regions of Europe and Asia. Because of the four emerging theaters of operation in cyberspace for such contingencies (see Figure S.1), strategic IW profoundly reduces the significance of distance with respect to the deployment and use of weapons. Therefore, battlefield C3I vulnerabilities may become less significant than vulnerabilities in the national infrastructure. Planning assumptions fundamental to current national military strategy are obsolescent. Consideration of these IW features should be accounted for in U.S. national military strategy.

Against this difficult projection and assessment situation, there is the ever-present risk that the United States could find itself in a crisis in the near term, facing the possibility of, or indications of, a strategic IW attack. When the president asks whether the United States is under IW attack—and, if so, by whom—and whether the U.S. military plan and strategy is vulnerable, a foot-shuffling "we don't know" will not be an acceptable answer.

Finally, however, it must be acknowledged that strategic IW is a very new concept that is presenting a wholly new set of problems. These problems may well yield to solution—but not without the intelligent and informed expenditure of energy, leadership, money, and other scarce resources that this study seeks to catalyze.

ACKNOWLEDGMENTS

We are grateful for the contributions of many people in government, industry, and within RAND to the conception and carrying out of this project. The following RAND staff deserve mention because of their extensive time investments and the shared insights that were so important in supporting the project's development: Richard O. Hundley, Robert H. Anderson, David Adamson, John Arquilla, Steven C. Bankes, Samuel Gardiner, Eugene C. Gritton, Anthony Hearn, Richard Mesic, Kevin O'Connell, and David F. Ronfeldt. We would also like to express special thanks to Kenneth E. deGraffenreid and Michelle K. Van Cleave of National Security Research, Inc.

Chapter One

WHAT IS "STRATEGIC INFORMATION WARFARE?"

INTRODUCTION

What is "Information Warfare?"

Ten years ago the answer to that question from a communications specialist, a code-breaker, or any other member of the U.S. military or intelligence communities might have been either "What?" or, with a little encouragement, "Oh, you mean command and control warfare on the battlefield and in the theater, jamming and that other electronic warfare stuff." Within most of the U.S. defense community today, you would still get an answer not far different from the above command and control warfare (C2W) or electronic warfare (EW) answer.

In many circles within the U.S. defense and broader international security community, however, the term information warfare is increasingly being used to encompass a broader set of information-age "warfare" concepts. These emerging new warfare concepts are directly tied to the prospect that the ongoing rapid evolution of cyberspace—the global information infrastructure (GII)—could bring both new opportunities and new vulnerabilities. This study focuses on one of these vulnerabilities: the prospect that this revolution could put at risk high-value national assets outside the traditional battlefield and theater of "over there" power projection in a fashion that affects both U.S. national military strategy and broader U.S. national security strategy.

We recognize that for some time the term information warfare in common usage will have no more than a general meaning, and one that is recognized to be inescapably dynamic. Information warfare, like the once-again evolving term "strategic warfare," is at a much too early stage of development or renewal to attempt to forge an agreed definition for the concept.

However, we think there is an emerging element of information warfare—one that appears to be common to almost all currently evolving uses of this term—that warrants identification and definition. We have labeled this emerging realm of conflict—wherein nations utilize cyberspace to affect strategic military operations and inflict damage on national information infrastructures—"strategic information warfare." As portrayed in Figure 1 and described in greater detail in the report that follows, we believe that strategic information warfare (in essence the intersection of evolving

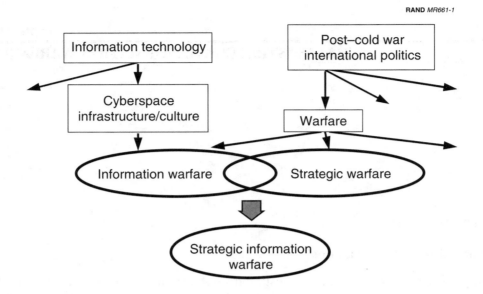

Figure 1—Strategic Information Warfare

information warfare and post–cold war "strategic warfare" concepts) warrants special recognition and attention as a legitimate new facet of warfare with profound implications for both U.S. military strategy and overall U.S. national security strategy.

The new cyberspace infrastructure and culture depicted in Figure 1 has, in recent years, evolved almost exclusively outside the military context (although the contribution of the Defense Department's ARPANET to the origins of the Internet are well known). As argued above, the emerging elements and characteristics of cyberspace by their very nature offer new opportunities for information warfare.

On a parallel track, there is the ongoing evolution in international politics, and within that context, the inevitable evolution of Clausewitz's warfare as an instrument of politics. In this context, new strategic interests are emerging for the United States and other nations, yielding new strategic dilemmas and new (and old) strategic targets against which to use leverage—including the threat of use of new (and old) kinds of strategic force. Thus, new strategic threats and new strategic vulnerabilities surface. It is increasingly clear, as this report seeks to portray, that the evolution in strategic warfare will include a dimension of cyberspace threats and vulnerabilities worthy of the label "strategic information warfare."

STUDY BACKGROUND

In January 1995, the Deputy Secretary of Defense established an Information Warfare (IW) Executive Board, supported by a comprehensive charter and organizational structure, to facilitate "the development and achievement of national information warfare goals." The intent of this initiative is to build on the current information warfare momentum within the Department of Defense, integrating and marshaling the many and various related efforts toward a path of common understanding of this subject in all of its manifestations, implications, and organizational roles and responsibilities.

In support of the IW Executive Board effort, RAND was asked by the Office of the Assistant Secretary of Defense (Command, Control, Communications, and Intelligence)—OASD(C3I)—to employ a methodology, previously developed by RAND for analyzing post–cold war international security strategy and policy problems, in a new project with the following specific purposes:

1. Define the major features of information warfare.

2. Sharpen senior executive focus on information warfare and understanding of its implications for national security.

3. Identify issues and assist policy direction of information warfare.

4. Engage national security and industry leadership on major implications of information warfare.

5. Coordinate with industry on future direction of related national security information systems strategy.

This report describes the results of that effort.

DEFENSE-ORIENTED TASKING FROM OASD(C3I)

In the project's terms of reference, RAND was asked to address what in traditional terms might be called the strategic *defensive* element (from a U.S. perspective) of what we came to label strategic information warfare for the reasons cited above. RAND was asked to avoid as much as possible getting into U.S. strategic *offensive* warfare prospects and capabilities.

The latter criterion was for the most part achieved, although it was difficult to keep participants from reflecting about the United States wielding offensive strategic warfare tools (in part as a consequence of mirror imaging) as they addressed possible cyberspace threats against which U.S. and allied strategic defenses might be required. Also, hewing to the criterion of avoiding U.S. offensive strategic information warfare capabilities altogether was admittedly somewhat like asking people to think only about U.S. strategic defenses against ballistic missiles and long-range bombers, and not to put such matters in the larger strategic warfare context that includes U.S. strategic offensive nuclear weapons.

As a partial outlet for participants' inclination to give some thought to the dimension of the United States on the offensive, the future crisis portions of the exercise methodology (see below) acknowledged the existence of a broad set of strategic information warfare decisions that a U.S. president would be making in a crisis, though these broader dimensions of the problem were not explored in the deliberations on possible near-term strategic information warfare initiatives. Thus, the findings and other perspectives presented below focus only on the defensive dimension of strategic information warfare.

Chapter Two

METHODOLOGY

THE "DAY AFTER . . ." EXERCISE METHODOLOGY

To carry out this study, RAND relied heavily on taking senior members of the U.S. national security community through an exercise-based framing and analysis of the strategic information warfare problem, examining a range of selected and diverse present and potential threats—and derivative policy and strategy implications—as discussed in detail below.

Through this process, exercise participants assessed possible adverse implications for information technology and practice and addressed unresolved issues associated with capabilities and limitations of current and planned systems and operational concepts. Participants were thus put in a position where they could more constructively help rationalize, stimulate, and direct the U.S. government and national-security-related telecommunications and information systems industries to move toward the objectives articulated in the IW Executive Board Charter.

RAND employed a previously developed exercise methodology, called "The Day After . . . ," as the vehicle for this framing and analysis of the IW problem. This methodology relies on a policy and strategy exploration exercise in which participants are presented with hypothetical future crises and asked to develop appropriate responses to such crises. During Step One of the exercise ("The Day of . . . "), participants are presented with a change or foreshadowed change in the strategic status quo. Step Two concerns "The Day After . . . "—the aftermath of a major strategic event at a later point in the same crisis context. Finally, Step Three returns to "The Day Before . . . " to consider measures that could be taken in the near future to avert such a crisis.

The methodology has previously been used for a variety of studies of evolving post–cold war strategic warfare problems in the areas of nuclear proliferation/counterproliferation and C3I. The recognition that strategic information warfare was of a comparable character and constituted a definable subset of the larger information warfare arena made it possible to exploit this available methodology. The methodology was also attractive because it provided an opportunity to explore operational and investment issues as well as policy and strategic issues. (See Appendix A for a description of the "Day After . . ." methodology.)

THE EXERCISE DESIGN PROCESS

It became clear in the very early stages of the study effort that there was a wholly new analytic realm emerging in the intersection of evolving strategic warfare and information warfare concepts. As a consequence, much early effort was devoted to (1) the development of a multidimensional analytical framework upon which, or along the dimensions of which, this newly emerging "strategic information warfare" problem could be presented and (2) a typology of strategic information scenarios for use in the "Day After . . ." methodology.

Major challenges in the design application of the "Day After . . ." exercise methodology include the choice and design of a first-generation strategic information warfare scenario, since no one scenario could illuminate all aspects of this problem. After considerable discussion, four hypothetical scenarios were examined for their plausibility and relevance to defense planning:

- **Persian Gulf Major Regional Contingency (MRC)-Type Crisis:** Iran seeks hegemony over the Persian Gulf region (circa 2000) by the overthrow of the Saudi Kingdom through the vehicle of an antiregime organization within Saudi Arabia. A major military crisis develops in the region with a decision by the U.S. government (USG) to deploy forces as part of a deterrent maneuver. Iran and its Saudi domestic "ally" conduct information warfare attacks on the Saudi government and the USG.

- **Strategic Challenge by China in the Far East:** China makes a very aggressive move toward regional dominance. The Taiwanese government declares "independence" (circa 2005). China conducts a robust combined-arms military operation, including the use of strategic information warfare techniques to deter a forceful U.S. political-military response.

- **Instability in Moscow:** A Russian Federation is ruled by a weak central government and largely in the thrall of several transcontinental crime organizations (TCOs). A major fissile material diversion is attempted by a Russian TCO to Iran (circa 1999). The Russian TCO makes extensive use of offensive and defensive IW techniques to further its objectives in the face of opposition from the United States, several major states within the European Union (EU), and the Russian government.

- **A Second Mexican Revolution:** There is an extrapolation of the current disturbances caused by the Chiapas rebellion in southern Mexico. A crisis occurs (circa 1998) in which the Mexican government faces major challenges from the Chiapas region as well as from antiregime movements in northern Mexico. The Mexican revolutionary movements and nongovernmental organization (NGO) allies in North America make extensive use of perception management techniques designed to dissuade the USG from taking any forceful political, economic, or military action to shore up the beleaguered Mexican regime.

We see the above set of scenarios as a good first cut at an exemplary set of strategic information warfare scenarios. We debated which scenario would be most effective at this point in the emergence of this new problem area, both as a teaching tool and as a means of further developing this overall subject analytically regarding *defensive* strategic information warfare. Table 1 provides elements of the evaluation approach that was used in comparing what fairly quickly became the two most attractive of the above scenarios in the light of the objectives of the study.

After consultation with members of the OASD(C3I) staff, the first of the above scenarios, we chose a more traditional "MRC-type" scenario in a traditional setting (i.e., the Persian Gulf), was chosen as likely to be most credible to senior participants in a first-generation strategic information warfare exercise. The choice was a balance between near-term plausibility and the requirement to play out a deliberately "exotic" turn-of-the-century information warfare scenario. We also felt that a plausible scenario that stressed the current assumptions of a standard MRC would usefully stimulate "new thinking."

The other scenarios listed above were all judged to have considerable intrinsic merit and be worthy of further exploration. Since the Persian Gulf power projection scenario is the strategic information warfare example that we lean so heavily on, it is fair to ask of this example, "Why is this 'strategic information warfare'?" What makes this scenario warrant such a strong characterization?

- First, because the potentially physically damaging attacks on the United States itself place the physical sanctuary of the continental United States at risk.

- Second, because one of the fundamental building blocks of the U.S. long-term military strategy is securing forces that can effectively suppress would-be regional hegemons before they are successful regionally and become would-be global hegemons.

- Third, because the conflict portrayed is seen as strategic warfare by Iran, the adversary. Whether a regional adversary is using information warfare techniques to fracture a coalition or undermine domestic support in the United States or

Table 1

Evaluation of Scenarios for Exercise

Factors	Saudi Arabia	China
1. What's at stake in the crisis	Oil	Rapidly evolving global competitor
2. Avoiding a strong nuclear shadow	Strength of nuclear shadow a variable	Inescapable large nuclear shadow
3. Exercise development risk (within time available)	Start from tested structure and context (from counterproliferation studies)	New context and untested structure
4. Participant "adaption" to scenario	Persian Gulf conflict familiar; time frame more immediate	Strategic context unfamiliar; time frame longer; better for 2nd exercise
5. Avoiding provoking strategic offensive IW	Not necessarily tempting	More tempting
6. Preparation for addressing pressing "Next Steps in IW" issues	Covers more issues	Covers fewer issues

Europe for intervention, it will be playing a strategic game that will force the United States into a strategic engagement as well.

• Fourth, when considering the strategic vulnerabilities and attacks that the United States and its allies might suffer, there is always the possibility that other strategic weapons—nuclear weapons, for example—might be either brandished or used outright.

Having chosen a scenario, we then faced the task of introducing a growing list of specific strategic information warfare threat elements (specific hacker threats, prospective infrastructure vulnerabilities, etc.) in a credible fashion into a fast-paced regional contingency crisis in the Gulf.

From this point on, the design of the exercise is in large measure a gradual introduction into the scenario of more and stronger elements of strategic information warfare, while turning down a comparable "rheostat" on the amount of traditional military conflict or brandishing of forces taking place.

The above phenomenon was in part a reflection of our growth in confidence in an evolving set of cyberspace-rooted vulnerabilities that, through this vetting process, fell in the category of potential problems that need to be brought forward for closer examination. At the same time, we admit to purposely bringing together in one concentrated period the candidate cyberspace threats that we came across on their "high end." In a more traditional sense, it might be called a look at the impact of the "greater-than-expected threat," although in this realm there is as yet no base of experience in which to root such concepts. (See Appendix B for a summary of the group responses to the June 3, 1995, exercise and Appendix C for the June 3 version of the exercise materials.)

We believe that the results that have emerged from this process—the schools of thought on substance and agenda described below that emerged from the exercise experience—constitute an important and unparalleled foundation on which to build the language and the analytical base to support presidential and other national-level decisionmaking that many agree are so badly needed.

In the latter context, we believe it is valid to say that the cyberspace threats that survived to the end of the exercise series constitute a good place to start in any risk assessment of threats to U.S. national security.

EXERCISE HISTORY

The exercise was developed and employed over a six-month period. After an initial research and design period, the project employed a series of different sets of participants (see Table 2) in a continually evolving exercise.

The first test series began with a small group of RAND researchers in Washington and progressed to include four-star military officers and assistant secretary–level officials representing departments and agencies from across the executive branch. Senior industry executives from large information-systems companies were included

Table 2

Exercise History

Dates	Participants
Feb 9	RAND Washington
Feb 23	RAND Santa Monica
Mar 16	Experts from DoD, intelligence community, industry, academia
Apr 10	Experts, retired Flag officers
Apr 22	DoD/industry: Two-star officers, DUSD/DASD,[a] senior VP level
May 13	DoD/industry: Four-star officers, USD/ASD, CEO[b] level
June 3	Expanded executive branch participation

[a]Department of the Under Secretary of Defense/Department of the Assistant Secretary of Defense.
[b]Chief Executive Officer.

throughout the series once it emerged from early testing. Over 170 individuals with significant experience in national security and military affairs, expert in various emerging and more-traditional dimensions of information warfare, participated. Participants represented various levels of industry, academia, the analytic and research communities, the intelligence community, national security policymakers, and the military services.

This process produced an opportunity to assess and analyze the perspectives of interested experts at high levels of government and industry regarding scenario plausibility, possible evolutions in threats and vulnerabilities, the phrasing of key policy issues, etc. It also provided an opportunity to identify emerging schools of thought and even, in some cases, rough consensus on key matters relating to strategic information warfare—as described in the following chapters.

Chapter Three

THE CHANGING FACE OF WAR

This chapter steps back and pictorially and analytically takes a broad look at information warfare, quickly closing in on the particular dimension of strategic information warfare, explaining in greater depth why we concluded that it was both necessary and desirable to identify and analyze this new face of warfare.

Figure 2 depicts a broad definition of information warfare, including those well-established aspects of IW that fall in the area of command and control warfare, especially in the context of the battlefield. As noted above, these aspects of IW are not new to U.S. military strategy, and the U.S. military establishment is exceptionally good at developing doctrine and conducting operations in this area.

Figure 2 also portrays the newer, emerging, and equally ominous facet of IW that we have labeled strategic information warfare. This facet includes a wider range of potential adversaries with the same selection of weapons, ranging from digits to dy-

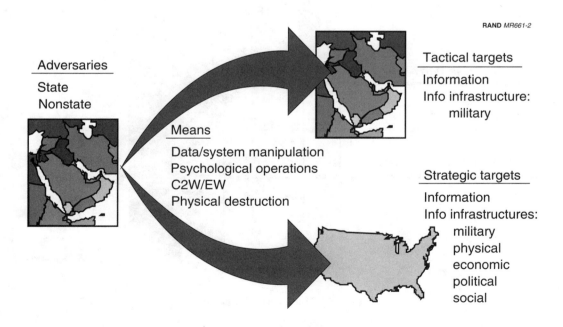

Figure 2—The Changing Face of War

namite. When these new strategic IW-armed actors point their weapons toward information-dependent infrastructures in the United States, such as the public switched network, financial systems, or air traffic control systems, IW inevitably takes on a strategic dimension.

Shown another way (see Figure 3), a complete description of modern information warfare ranges from well-understood, tactical command-and-control warfare (either as precursor conflict or in the context of a large conventional war) to what is newer—a more penetrating kind of conflict that reaches the center of the U.S. homeland. The implication here is ominous: IW threatens the United States as sanctuary.

As the various groups worked their way through the hypothetical crisis presented, it became clear that each participant could deal more easily with some aspects of information warfare than with others—participants naturally responded most easily with what they knew best. Information-based conflict in the region (C2W in the MRC) presented minor challenges. But, when the information warfare campaign was brought to the U.S. and allies' heartlands, the MRC became almost irrelevant. Attention was spread from one or two traditional campaign areas (or theaters) "over there" to a total of *four* operational theaters as portrayed in Figure 4, including "here."

When responding to information warfare, military strategy can thus no longer focus just on support to and operations in the MRC. It must also examine IW implications on U.S. and allies' strategic infrastructures—military, physical, economic, political, and social—that depend upon information systems and information support.

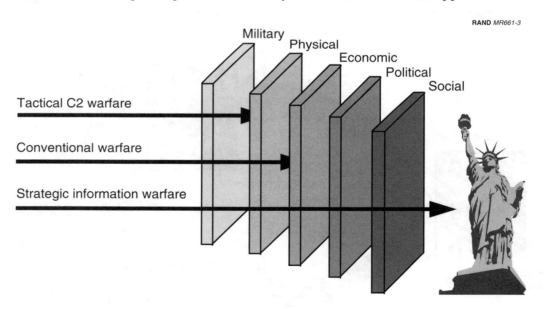

RAND *MR661-3*

Figure 3—The Loss of Sanctuary

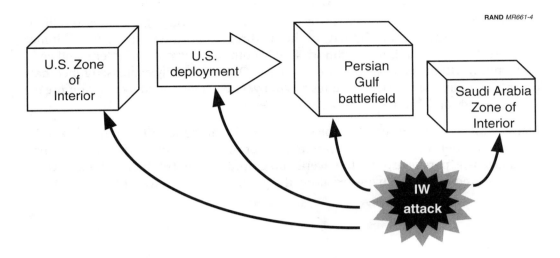

RAND MR661-4
U.S. Zone of Interior
U.S. deployment
Persian Gulf battlefield
Saudi Arabia Zone of Interior
IW attack

Figure 4—Four Strategic IW "Theaters of Operation"

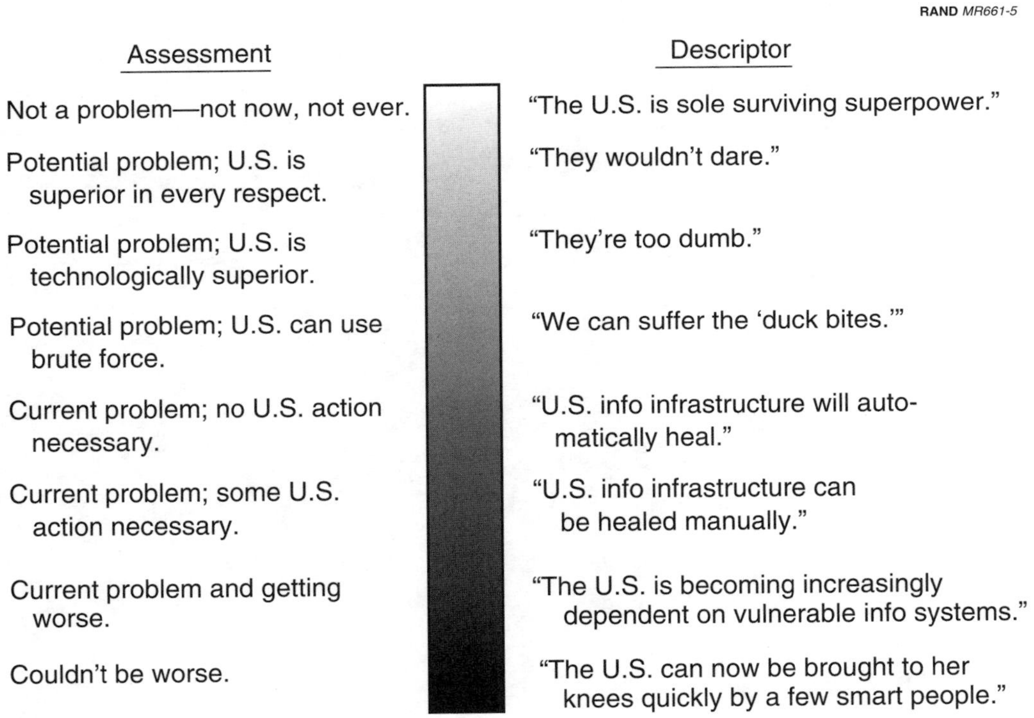

RAND MR661-5
Assessment
Descriptor
Not a problem—not now, not ever.
"The U.S. is sole surviving superpower."
Potential problem; U.S. is superior in every respect.
"They wouldn't dare."
Potential problem; U.S. is technologically superior.
"They're too dumb."
Potential problem; U.S. can use brute force.
"We can suffer the 'duck bites.'"
Current problem; no U.S. action necessary.
"U.S. info infrastructure will automatically heal."
Current problem; some U.S. action necessary.
"U.S. info infrastructure can be healed manually."
Current problem and getting worse.
"The U.S. is becoming increasingly dependent on vulnerable info systems."
Couldn't be worse.
"The U.S. can now be brought to her knees quickly by a few smart people."

Figure 5—A Broad Spectrum of Perspectives

As participants were immersed in the scenario, they expressed a wide and telling range of perspectives on the gravity of the IW threat as portrayed in Figure 5. Some confidently stated that information warfare is nothing new, not a problem, and certainly not worth the expense of another nickel. Others publicly expressed relief that the infrastructure of the United States has not yet been devastated by one or more of the thousands of IW attacks it has already suffered.

Many of the participants came to the exercises with only a modest amount of experience in considering information warfare problems. In the great majority of groups, the consensus perspective on the overall magnitude of the IW threat almost invariably appeared to move downward along the graph of Figure 5 over the course of the exercise.

Chapter Four

DEFINING FEATURES OF STRATEGIC INFORMATION WARFARE

The exercises highlighted seven defining features of strategic information warfare that distinguish it from other forms of conflict and pose new challenges for the U.S. government, American society, and U.S. allies. These features, which constitute highly effective avenues along which to explore the strategic IW problem, warrant special attention:

- **Low entry cost.** *The price to develop a high-performance IW capability is low and is available to a wide range of participants.* Unlike previous high-performance weapons technologies, new potential information warfare weapons can be developed by skilled individuals or groups residing anywhere within the GII.

- **Blurred traditional boundaries.** *Traditional boundaries between nations and segments of society and government—and even conceptual definitions such as that of the nation-state—are blurred.* Distinctions between public and private interests are compromised by growing interaction within the information infrastructure. The explosive global growth and exploitation of the Internet show a wide-open, unregulated frontier characteristic of this infrastructure. Within this new frontier, which is characterized by pluralism and growing numbers of factions, there is wide opportunity for criminal and/or warfare-type activity.

- **Perception Management.** *Perception management may play an expanded role.* Although the organized and systematic use of deception techniques has powerful historical antecedents, new information-based techniques may provide perception manipulators a powerful set of new tools.

- **Strategic intelligence.** *Strategic intelligence presents a fundamental new challenge.* Newly identified IW threats and vulnerabilities will necessitate a thorough review of classical intelligence collection and analysis methods. A new type of strategic intelligence analytic field may need to be developed.

- **Tactical warning and attack assessment.** *Tactical warning and attack assessment (TW/AA) constitute another new challenge.* Given the diversity and subtlety of various defense and attack techniques within the information infrastructure, a new type of TW/AA will have to be devised to detect and differentiate between mistake, accident, deployment of software agents designed for espionage, and the predeployment of software weapons. TW/AA will require monitoring all elements of the GII, national information infrastructure (NII), and defense information infrastructure (DII) to detect surveillance, penetration, disruption, and weapon predeployment activities.

- **Building and sustaining coalitions.** *Increased reliance on coalition allies brings increased vulnerabilities.* Future major regional contingencies will involve militarily and geographically important coalition partners. These allies may have special vulnerabilities to emerging IW attack techniques—and concerns about U.S. vulnerabilities—that an adversary might exploit to undermine coalition participation.

- **Vulnerability of the U.S. homeland.** *The U.S. homeland may be vulnerable to a new strategic threat.* Given the increased reliance of the U.S. economy and society on high-performance computer networks, U.S. infrastructures represent a new set of "strategic" targets. Threats against key NII targets may have an extremely coercive value, while outright attacks may have a powerful disruptive effect on the national decisionmaking authority. U.S. borders will not provide sanctuary from this kind of conflict.

As we presented and further developed each of these essential features in the context of the evolving exercise, we came to appreciate in far greater depth their individual consequences. The outcome of this process, summarized in Table 3, convinced us that we had been able to capture in a comprehensible fashion those aspects of strategic information warfare that distinguish it from other new forms of conflict.

The following material describes in detail each of these features as well as how they were incorporated into the exercise. Further, the material provides a summary of preliminary findings or insights about various exercise teams' reactions to these features.

Table 3

Strategic Information Warfare from Features to Consequences

Features	Consequences
1. *Low entry cost* dramatically multiplies threat.	Anybody can attack.
2. *Blurred traditional boundaries* create new problems.	You may not know who is under attack, by whom . . . or who's in charge.
3. *Perception management* has expanded role.	You may not know what is real.
4. *Strategic intelligence* is not yet available.	You may not know who your adversaries will be . . . or what their intentions or capabilities will be.
5. *Tactical warning and attack assessment* are extremely difficult.	You may not know you are under attack, who is attacking . . . or how.
6. *Building and sustaining coalitions* is more complicated.	You may depend on others who are vulnerable.
7. *Vulnerability of the U.S. homeland* may give adversaries leverage.	You lose the United States as sanctuary.

LOW ENTRY COST

Feature Description

The occurrence most fundamental to the emergence of information warfare is the confluence of low-cost microcomputing and the exploitation of ever more complex communication networks in order to gain, for example, increased efficiency in the management of the flow of data, material, and other "goods" and related information from various producers and consumers. This circumstance leads directly to significantly increased numbers, kinds, and capabilities of potential IW adversaries. Another aspect of the low-entry-cost feature is the rapidly increasing complexity of the information infrastructures and the consequent impact of this complexity on other features, such as blurred boundaries, strategic intelligence, and tactical warning/attack assessment.

There is a powerful commercial imperative to ensure that the emerging system of cyberspace networks operates with increased efficiency so that inventories of any data and/or material commodity can be exploited with less need for the maintenance of large inventories that compensate for uncertainties about supply and demand. This substitution of "efficiency for mass" in many cases unfortunately leads to new types of vulnerabilities to attack—especially in the early (and during any other) dynamic stages of a network's evolution (more the rule than the exception in much of cyberspace). This rapidly evolving phenomenon provides a malevolent and competent cyberspace actor with potential near-speed-of-light access to a wide range of national "strategic targets" within the GII.

In this situation, many advanced and interconnected networks can be subjected to attack by a range of entities including skilled individuals; actors that are not states, such as transnational criminal organizations; and states with a well-trained cadre of "cyberspace warriors." The key ingredients are access and mastery over, for example, a particular data file, data management system, or flow control system—in a context where key information infrastructure databases and management and control systems are increasingly interconnected.

The most dramatic example of this phenomenon is the explosive growth of the Internet, in which tens of millions of users exploit a global communications network with access to tens of thousands of databases that are provided little or no protection against "unauthorized" entry. In essence, the Internet has some of the features of much of the land rapidly opened for cattle grazing during the late 19th century. This "Wild West" metaphor is apt since there is now a public debate as to whether users of the Internet should readily acquire the cyberspace equivalent of barbed wire—database access protection through encryption or other techniques.

Encryption at the entry points to various databases and to act as message authenticators of appropriate system users is a plausible means to increasing the entry price for certain classes of "amateur" and low-technology cyberspace attackers ("rogue hackers"). In fact some participants in the exercise strongly believed that the solution to much of the vulnerability of a future national information infrastructure was at hand with a laissez-faire approach to the diffusion of encryption technology to personal, commercial, nonstate, and state users. Whether such an "answer" to the low entry price would produce a very high domestic law enforcement/foreign national security "price" was well beyond the scope of this effort. At a minimum, we note that one of the possible consequences of the rapid diffusion of encryption technology would be to further increase the difficulty of domestic and foreign intelligence collection institutions in monitoring, much less identifying, the source of future cyberspace attackers. The problem of devising a credible TW/AA system would be made even worse by widespread encryption (see below); strategic warning would be made more difficult as well.

How This Feature Was Explored in the Exercise

One of the challenges of designing a credible scenario for the turn of the century was creating a picture of the major features of the national and global information infrastructure. As is well understood by many students of the phenomenon of cyberspace, we had to make some assumptions about the nature of the U.S. infrastructure and its vulnerability to cyberspace-type attacks. As described in greater detail in the background material for the exercise (see Appendix C), the major low-entry-cost features that were developed included the impact of

- The cellular revolution
- The expansion of the Internet and the World Wide Web
- The growth of electronic commerce
- The growth in activist use of the NII and GII
- The increased DoD reliance on the commercial switched telephone and public data systems
- The use of computer worms and viruses.

Participants' Reactions/Perspectives

Over the exercise series, almost all participants accepted the plausibility of strategic IW attack options with relatively low entry cost and attackers potentially located anywhere within cyberspace.

Next Steps/Step Three

Some participants did believe that the entry price to many of the IW attack options posited within the various scenarios could be substantially raised through USG toleration of an approach that allowed individuals and institutions to deny easy access to networks and control systems through the exploitation of new software encryption techniques. Other participants in the exercises acknowledged that widespread encryption might mitigate some threats but that this approach would not remove direct physical attack or other threats to an internetted system by a corrupted insider (systems operator).

Aside from acknowledging the plausibility of low-entry-cost threats, most participants believed that this new dimension of warfare would require a new type of risk assessment. Practical approaches to this assessment are discussed below.

Figure 6 summarizes the key elements of this feature.

RAND MR661-6

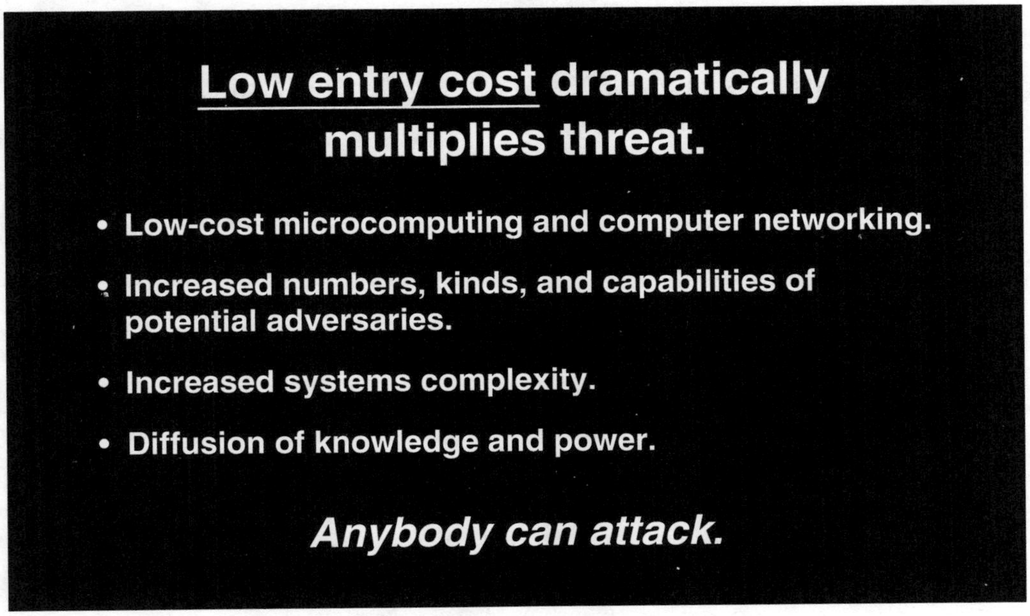

Low entry cost dramatically multiplies threat.

- Low-cost microcomputing and computer networking.
- Increased numbers, kinds, and capabilities of potential adversaries.
- Increased systems complexity.
- Diffusion of knowledge and power.

Anybody can attack.

Figure 6—Low-Entry-Cost Summary

BLURRED TRADITIONAL BOUNDARIES

Feature Description

One of the most significant features of the development of a global informational infrastructure (and subordinate national infrastructures) is the blurring of clear geographical, bureaucratic, jurisdictional, and even conceptual boundaries associated with traditional national security issues. For example, boundaries defining a sovereign state will become increasingly blurred. Not unlike the nation-states' loss of control over the current global financial and monetary markets, the increased interconnection of the U.S. national information infrastructure with global cyberspace inescapably diminishes national sovereignty.

Among the most striking aspects of this blurred-boundaries phenomenon is the disappearance of the ability to make any kind of clear distinction between foreign and domestic sources of IW threats to the safety of the republic. This blurring of boundaries greatly exacerbates institutional tensions between the U.S. national security and law enforcement communities.

Another blurring phenomenon is the virtual disappearance in numerous circumstances of clear distinctions between different levels of anti-state activity in the spectrum from crime to military conflict. Without a clear geographical distinction between foreign and domestic sources of anti-U.S. activity, there is the increased prospect that activities associated with traditional espionage, crime, and "acts of war" will be very difficult to identify. With the prospect that infrastructures can be attacked via cyberspace, there is an increased likelihood that nation-states weaker than the United States in the traditional instruments of military and economic power will employ individuals and/or TCOs to conduct "strategic criminal operations" whose actual origins ("Who gave the order?") will prove very hard to identify.

Other examples of blurred traditional distinctions include those between public and private, military and commercial, and strategic and tactical. A final example is the blurring in numerous circumstance of "weapons effects"—the considerable uncertainty about actual versus intended "weapons effects," especially the problems of unknown collateral damage within and between infrastructures from any specific action taken.

The consequence of blurred boundaries is the very real possibility that if attacked, the United States may not sense what is under attack. Similarly, it will not be immediately clear what agency or segment of society should be responsible for taking charge of any attack response.

How This Feature Was Explored in the Exercise

As developed in detail in the exercise itself (see Appendix C) the major blurred-boundaries features that were explored included (1) an ambiguous relationship between the Saudi domestic opposition (a hypothetical nongovernmental organization promoting "Islamic democracy") and Iran and (2) the blurring of domestic and foreign interest boundaries within the United States (through the appearance of a powerful conflict mediation–oriented organization that orchestrates an anti-interventionist campaign). The latter was modeled after some of the NGO activity that has already occurred on the Internet between the organization leading the Mexican Chiapas rebellion and U.S. "peace activist" organizations.

The scenario also heightened the sense of uncertainty about the distinction between domestic crime (terrorist) acts and "acts of war" through incidents such as (1) major failures of the public switched network (PSN) within the United States and Saudi Arabia and (2) major acts of IW sabotage of uncertain origin against key infrastructure control systems.

Participants' Reactions/Perspectives

In the early versions of the exercise (see earlier discussion of exercise history), the scenario presented posited much higher levels of military violence and a more overt military threat from Iran during the escalating crisis. For example, the initial exercise scenarios described a circumstance in the Persian Gulf region in which Iran had already taken advantage of the domestic turmoil inside Saudi Arabia and was moving military forces into the major Gulf city of Dhahran at the request of domestic opponents to the Saudi kingdom. These initial test exercises also played out U.S. domestic IW events with a somewhat clearer connection with Iran. Because the source and character of the political and military threat to the vital interests were rendered less ambiguous, many groups during these exercises were prepared to recommend that the United States take major military action against Iran. Put simply, the boundaries between peace and war had not been sufficiently blurred.

In response to this phenomenon, the scenario was modified in subsequent exercises. The "rheostat" for overt military action committed by Iran was turned down. Simultaneously, the level of domestic crisis was dramatically increased with a much more energetic domestic opposition led by a powerful "anti-interventionist" nongovernmental organization. In response to this increased blurring of the distinction between a domestic law enforcement crisis and a foreign national security crisis, many exercise groups found it much more difficult to recommend decisive military action even after the crisis had escalated in a fashion described by the exercise scenario.

Adding to the "paralytic effect" on some groups' decision process was the widespread uncertainty generated by major incidents in both the United States and Saudi Arabia that involved the use of IW techniques by an imperfectly identified perpetrator.

This debate about how to respond to ambiguous domestic IW-type events spilled over in the group debates about the appropriateness and effectiveness of any U.S. response in kind taken against Iran during this crisis. Within several groups, there was intense debate as to how the United States could effectively deter further IW attacks against key elements of the domestic infrastructure when there was considerable uncertainty about the immediate and longer-term consequences of any offensive IW attack operations threatened or taken by the United States.

Most groups in the operational exercises expressed profound frustration with a scenario that posited a U.S. law enforcement and intelligence community that provided such incomplete information about the origin of the more heinous IW events presented (specifically, train and aircraft crashes).

Next Steps/Step Three

The exercise groups frequently engaged in a vigorous debate between those who advocated a "merger" of domestic law enforcement and intelligence functions to meet the strategic IW challenge and those who thought that the distinction between domestic law enforcement and foreign intelligence collection should be clearly maintained. Advocates of a merger of the law enforcement and intelligence agencies believed that the kind of IW-type events described in the scenario compelled the USG to take "extraordinary action" to provide the national command authorities with both better intelligence and a more integrated action plan to respond to a form of warfare that blurred the distinction between domestic and foreign concerns. Opponents citing traditional civil rights concerns noted that many of the IW events within the continental United States could be labeled domestic acts of terrorism and treated in a fashion not unlike the law enforcement response to the World Trade Center and Oklahoma City bombings.

Figure 7 summarizes the key elements of this feature.

RAND *MR661-7*

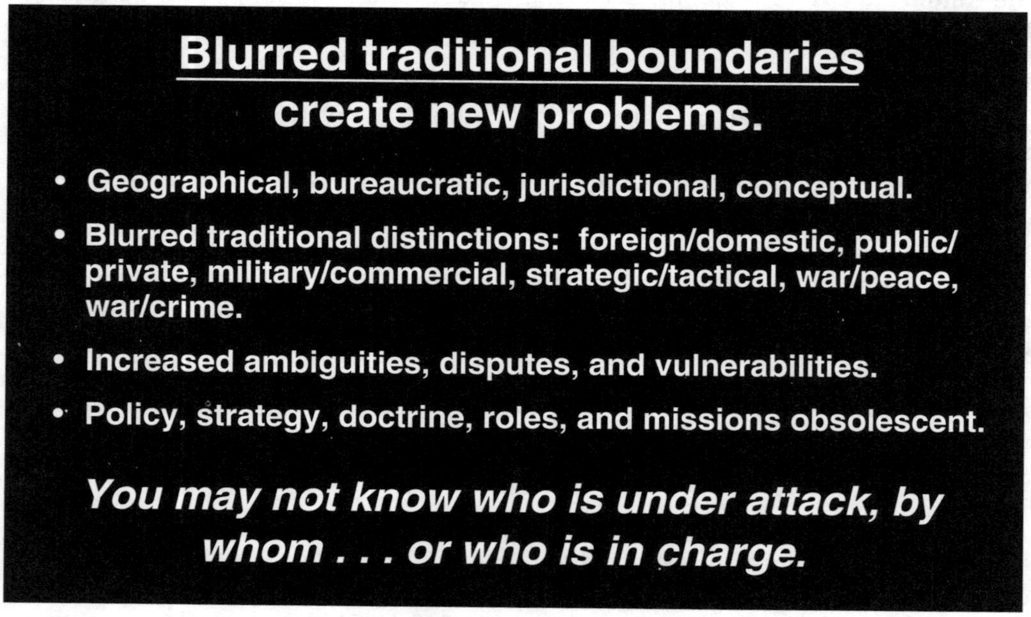

Blurred traditional boundaries create new problems.

- Geographical, bureaucratic, jurisdictional, conceptual.
- Blurred traditional distinctions: foreign/domestic, public/private, military/commercial, strategic/tactical, war/peace, war/crime.
- Increased ambiguities, disputes, and vulnerabilities.
- Policy, strategy, doctrine, roles, and missions obsolescent.

You may not know who is under attack, by whom . . . or who is in charge.

Figure 7—Blurred Traditional Boundaries Summary

PERCEPTION MANAGEMENT

Feature Description

As cyberspace evolves, entry cost decreases, and the boundaries of national sovereignty are blurred, there will be increased opportunity for adept nonstate and state actors to manipulate information that is key to perceptions.

To begin with, the Internet and its likely turn-of-the-century commercial competitors provide a distribution network for "propaganda" generated by a wide range of actors. Recent events in Mexico during the Chiapas rebellion provide a concrete example of how the Internet can be exploited to mobilize both media attention and political support within Mexico and the rest of North America for political and economic goals of the antiregime organizations. In the wake of the Oklahoma City bombing, there is increased evidence that a variety of paramilitary organizations—the "militia movement"—have utilized the Internet to build political support and provide local organizations with a wide range of information and disinformation. Political action groups and nongovernment organizations would be able to utilize the Internet to mobilize political support, especially against a U.S. administration that chooses to employ military force in a crisis fraught with uncertainty and potential domestic controversy.

Further, there is the possibility that the "facts" of an event can be powerfully manipulated via text, audio, and video (such as the use of advanced video techniques to manipulate images). In particular, such techniques may allow a wide variety of actors to conduct sophisticated perception management or public diplomacy campaigns designed to undermine domestic support for a particular course of action taken by the USG. These kinds of campaigns pose problems not only for the government but also for the media as an institution in their search for "accurate coverage."

The direct consequence of this feature is that U.S. decisionmakers and/or the American public may not know what is real.

How This Feature Was Explored in the Exercise

The methodology of the "Day After . . ." exercise does not provide a ready "playing field" for the more technologically innovative concepts of perception management. Rather, the exercise scenario was designed to highlight the role that powerful NGOs might play in future political military crisis scenarios. In this regard, the scenario appeared to capture the potential role of major domestic opponents to U.S. and Saudi government plans and policies—and by implication the "perceptions" that such opponents might seek to "manage."

Participants' Reactions/Perspectives

Most participants in the operational exercises took the prospect of major domestic opposition very seriously. For a number of groups, the presence of a powerful domestic opponent to the Saudi government undermined their confidence in any overt political military plan designed to shore up the Saudi government even though it might be a victim of Iranian subversion and coercion simultaneously. In response to the prospect that the U.S. president would face a powerful and well-organized domestic opposition, several groups gave considerable attention to the crafting of a public diplomacy strategy, including the suggestion by one group that the administration should make its case on the Internet as well as through traditional media outlets.

Next Steps/Step Three

Among the participants in the operational exercises, there was no support for any extraordinary maneuver by the administration of a "Seize control of the media and the Internet!" character. Rather, there was an acknowledgment that a U.S. administration might have a daunting task in shaping and sustaining domestic support for any action that called for U.S. military intervention in a regional crisis marked by a high degree of ambiguity and uncertainty in the IW realm.

Figure 8 summarizes the key elements of this feature.

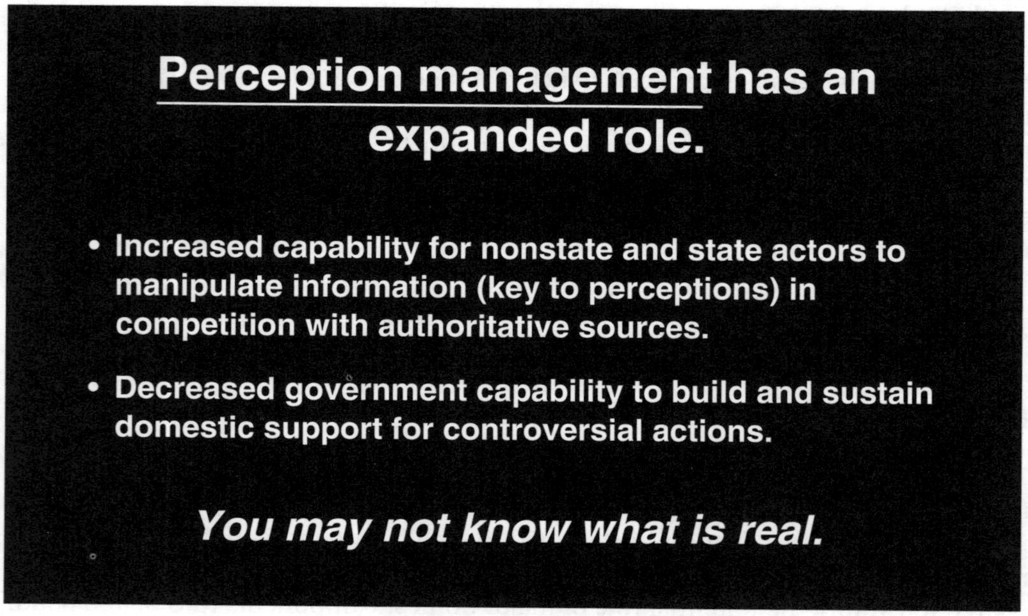

Figure 8—Perception Management Summary

STRATEGIC INTELLIGENCE

Feature Description

Because of the features of low entry price and blurred boundaries, the U.S. intelligence community may face great difficulties in providing timely and credible strategic intelligence to the executive branch about current and future IW threats—a challenge that many of the exercise participants strongly emphasized.

Targets for collection of intelligence will clearly be far more difficult to identify. The classical geostrategic approach of focusing on specific nation-states as "threats" has become obsolescent.   Intelligence collection targets will now include nongovernmental organizations, TCOs, and actors that are not nation-states. The weight and significance of a particular threat will depend upon an assessment of both the capability of potential cyberspace attackers, their intentions, and the vulnerability of a particular target set. The capability of a particular attacker may be obcured by the very dynamic nature of cyberspace telecommunications, microprocessor hardware/software, and defensive techniques, e.g., encryption. This infrastructure will include a wide spectrum of the elements of a turn-of-the-century technologically and economically advanced society. These infrastructure elements include (1) the PSN, (2) oil and gas pipelines, (3) electric power grids, (4) transportation control systems, (5) the Federal Funds Transfer System, (6) various bank transfer systems, and (7) the health care system. While some of the vulnerabilities of these infrastructure elements are well understood, many are not.

It will be extremely difficult for the intelligence community to develop and maintain a stable list of potential threats. The overall global environment has moved to a much more dynamic multipolar as opposed to a static bipolar structure. The United States will have to deal with a wide range of great powers, including Japan, Russia, China, India, the major states of the European Union, and other increasingly important nations like Indonesia and Brazil in circumstances of cooperation and competition. Depending upon the specific geostrategic and economic circumstance, the USG may find one or more traditional allies acting as economic rivals. Further, the USG may face the difficult task of sorting competing policy objectives with military peers who have nationalist ambitions contrary to U.S. strategic goals. On a smaller scale, the United States may face smaller state actors, multinational corporations, and TCOs that are able and prepared to challenge U.S. strategic interests. Setting collection and analytical resources and investment priorities will prove very difficult for the leadership of the national intelligence community.

Consequences of the strategic intelligence problem include the possibility that the United States may not know who its adversaries will be or what their intentions and capabilities will be.

How This Feature Was Explored in the Exercise

In the design of the exercise scenario, it was posited that the USG would *not* make any comprehensive changes in how it organized its current law enforcement and intelligence community structure during the next five years. The only major change posited was the appearance of a Domestic Counterterrorism Center that would have intelligence analytical capabilities but rely upon domestic law enforcement and the intelligence community structure for collection. The scenario presented a postulated "future history" of a variety of incidents that strongly hinted of enhanced IW-type capabilities, including the penetration of government command and control networks, large diversions of bank funds, and a series of aggressive IW events of uncertain origin targeted against U.S. domestic and Saudi targets.

Participants' Reactions/Perspectives

Participants in the operational exercises expressed considerable frustration that in this scenario the intelligence community was so ineffective in providing precise strategic intelligence about the source and nature of future IW threats, especially those that might be developed by Iran.

Next Steps/Step Three

Although there was a wide consensus among participants that at least some part of the intelligence community would have to be reorganized to meet the strategic IW intelligence challenge, there was no consensus on how this should be done. Basically, there were two schools of thought. One group believed that some type of interagency structure was needed to allow for the coordinated collection and analysis of "domestic" and "foreign" intelligence. The second group strongly opposed any institutional commingling of domestic law enforcement and foreign intelligence tasks.

Figure 9 summarizes the key elements of this feature.

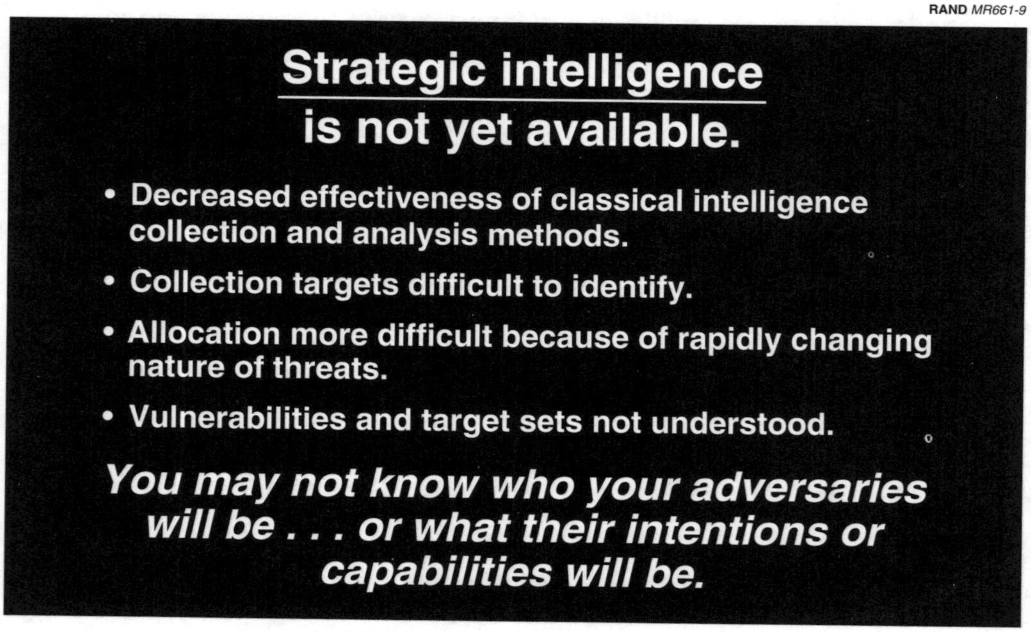

Figure 9—Strategic Intelligence Summary

TACTICAL WARNING AND ATTACK ASSESSMENT

Feature Description

Flowing from the inherent difficulty of conducting strategic intelligence, the time pressure of a crisis makes the challenge of TW/AA even more daunting. There is a real prospect that for a given attack or situation, the national command authorities will be presented with strongly conflicting assessments from different law enforcement and intelligence community organizations.

An attacker using cyberspace weapons is able to conduct strategic operations at unprecedented speeds and withdraw to the confines of cyberspace. Finding the "smoking gun" in a timely fashion will be very difficult if not impossible, especially in the context of a severe crisis in which there is little time for a more traditional law enforcement-type investigation.

Given the increased complexity of a variety of communications networks, database management systems, and systems controls, some events will be the product of bad luck or bad design. Further, there are likely to be strategic offensive measures in which systems are penetrated and compromised over the course of a multiyear "preparation of a battlefield." Much of this activity may be misdiagnosed.

The result of this feature is that the United States may not know an attack is under way, who is attacking, or how the attack is being conducted.

How This Feature Was Explored in the Exercise

This aspect of the IW crisis environment was successfully captured by the exercises through inclusion of the following types of events: (1) major failures of the PSN within the United States and Saudi Arabia and (2) major acts of sabotage through software attacks on key control systems, including ground and air transportation systems for which identification of the perpetrators of these "IW" events remains ambiguous.

Participants' Reactions/Perspectives

The teams expressed concerns about the basic ability of the United States to manage escalation in an IW conflict in an environment of a great deal of uncertainty. One team debated the question of whether the use of IW techniques by the adversary was an act of war and therefore whether the country could respond with all feasible military options. One group gained a consensus after some debate that it would be feasible and desirable to merge the intelligence community and FBI assets to help develop an appropriate threat assessment during this escalating crisis.

Another expressed concern was that, in the scenario, the Iranians (and their allies) might not be at the limits of their capability to conduct even more damaging IW-type attacks. In this case, the United States might risk increased retaliation with uncertain outcomes if it reacted too strongly against the current actions. One team debated this issue in such terms as the following: "Is the United States under attack and if so, by whom? Why is there a lack of emergency response plans?" They decided to close the fire walls of a postulated "minimum essential information infrastructure" and felt it was important to probe this new information infrastructure prior to its activation to understand its vulnerabilities.

Overall, most groups were very cautious about recommending any dramatic act of military escalation during the crisis phase (Step One) of the exercise (see Appendix D).

Many participants of the operational exercise expressed the view that the "failure of the intelligence community" in this scenario to provide effective TW/AA seriously inhibited, if not crippled, the administration's capacity to take decisive action against the would-be regional hegemon, Iran.

Next Steps/Step Three

Similar to the debate over what to do about the dilemmas posed by the strategic intelligence challenge, the participants split between those who were prepared to consider a more radical mix of domestic law enforcement and foreign intelligence institutions and those strongly opposed to any commingling.

Figure 10 summarizes the key elements of this feature.

RAND MR661-10

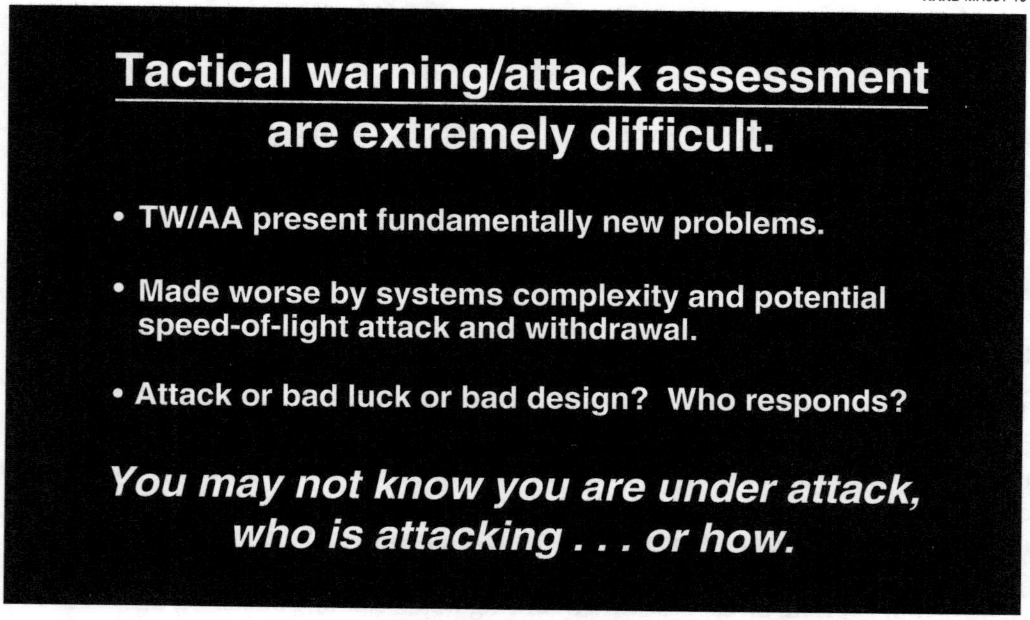

Tactical warning/attack assessment are extremely difficult.

- TW/AA present fundamentally new problems.

- Made worse by systems complexity and potential speed-of-light attack and withdrawal.

- Attack or bad luck or bad design? Who responds?

You may not know you are under attack, who is attacking . . . or how.

Figure 10—Tactical Warning and Attack Assessment Summary

BUILDING AND SUSTAINING COALITIONS

Feature Description

A U.S. administration will find that building and sustaining foreign coalitions to support forceful action against future international hostilities will be very difficult, a situation that may be exacerbated by IW issues. Many allies may themselves have a high degree of vulnerability to IW-type attacks on their core infrastructure. Several factors enhance this difficulty. First, important allies and/or friends of the United States will face the same daunting problem of maintaining reliable strategic intelligence and a tactical warning and attack assessment capability. Once serious information conflict is under way, coalition sustenance becomes increasingly challenging as allies are engulfed in the fog of IW. Acute problems in executing a coalition plan could also occur if one of the partners is found to be a "weak link in the chain" due to IW vulnerabilities.

Second, many countries may have acute vulnerabilities in key sectors (e.g., communications, energy, transportation, and financial) that an adversary might attack to undermine coalition participation. Such vulnerabilities are likely to be especially acute during the early phase of these countries' exploitation of the information technology revolution when attention will focus more on acquiring capability than on ensuring system security. New systems procured outside the country (in the name of early and cost-effective commercial deployment) may prove especially vulnerable. A case in point is the rapid diffusion of cellular telephone systems in countries that lack the traditional land line-wire infrastructure. Current-generation cellphones are potentially very vulnerable to monitoring and interference and theft of subscriber identification numbers. New-generation cellphones will be less vulnerable, but the cost of a generation turnover may deter rapid change in lower-income countries.

Conversely, another concern is that tentative coalition partners who would need military assistance may demand assurances that a U.S. deployment plan to their region is not vulnerable to IW disruption before they commit to coalition participation.

U.S. future dependence in conflict on allies and coalition partners that are potentially vulnerable (possibly in unique ways) to strategic IW is a consequence with significant impact on national security strategy, which implicitly assumes their timely and stalwart support.

How This Feature Was Explored in the Exercise

During the operational exercise scenario, this issue was illuminated by the description of a series of events taking place worldwide that provided the participants with a profound sense of uncertainty about the character of the attack. Especially telling were ambiguous IW-type events that unfolded in Egypt, which undermined that government's support for a U.S. decision to send forces to shore up a beleaguered Saudi regime. Similarly, in the scenario the highly energetic domestic opposition within Saudi Arabia conducts extensive IW-type actions in an effort to undermine the Saudi government.

Participants' Reactions/Perspectives

For many participants in the exercises, this feature of the IW scenario was one of the most worrisome. While acknowledging that a very important ally of the United States was in deep trouble due to a "combined arms" attack, several groups considered attempting to broker a political arrangement that would incorporate the emerging domestic Saudi political forces in a new internal Saudi political arrangement to secure the territorial sovereignty of Saudi Arabia in the face of Iranian hegemonic aggressiveness. Overall, a majority of the participants and groups decided against taking any action that would appear to undermine the current Saudi regime. There was a consensus that such an action would be seen as the "betrayal of a loyal allied regime" and could facilitate the Iranians' gaining hegemony over the Persian Gulf region. In the end of the group debates, a major fraction agreed in principle that the United States should provide the Saudi government with defensive measures to protect itself and the Saudi national information infrastructure from future IW-type attacks.

Next Steps/Step Three

Other than acknowledging this problem, none of the groups made concrete recommendations on steps or policies to enhance the U.S. capability to provide IW-type defensive measures to an ally under IW-type attacks, though as noted above, the desirability of pursuing such actions was readily acknowledged.

Figure 11 summarizes the key elements of this feature.

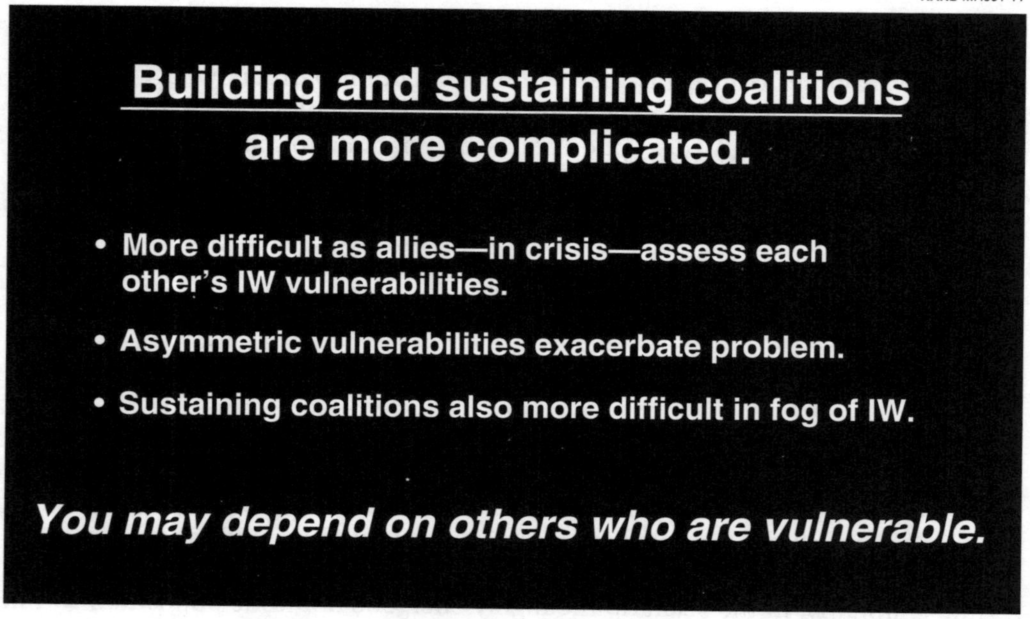

Figure 11—Building and Sustaining Coalitions Summary

VULNERABILITY OF THE U.S. HOMELAND

Feature Description

To improve the overall efficiency of the U.S. economy, various key infrastructure networks (see examples cited above) will become increasingly reliant on ever more sophisticated network control systems. As a consequence, these infrastructure elements will present strategically very lucrative targets.

In this context, protecting the U.S. infrastructure from cyberspace weapon attacks by threatening retaliation appears extremely problematic. As noted, there is likely to be a great deal of ambiguity about the source of many strategic information warfare events. Opponents of the United States will make much of the opportunity to conduct a damaging campaign that does not invite "immediate and massive retaliation." Further, U.S. strategists will have to devise a coherent concept of escalation and escalation control. This may prove daunting when there is considerable uncertainty about the actual "lethal radius" of a particular cyberspace weapon, much less the collateral damage caused by the successful attack on a particular national information infrastructure.

Aside from the possibility that future opponents will attack the infrastructure of the United States in response to U.S. military action taken in a particular Eurasian theater of operation, there is also the possibility that this opponent will be able to exploit cyberspace to manipulate the U.S. domestic perception of the conflict.

The U.S. "Zone of the Interior" is thus potentially very vulnerable to an IW attack—and for the foreseeable future it will be very difficult to prove the contrary. The consequence of this feature is inescapable: The U.S. sanctuary is lost against this new face of strategic conflict.

How This Feature Was Explored in the Exercise

As noted above, this scenario posits a continuation of trends already under way. Within the next five years, the telecommunications and control networks of the entire U.S. economic infrastructure will become increasingly interconnected. In response to the possible vulnerability of this national infrastructure, the exercise scenario posited that a minimum essential information infrastructure (MEII) might ensure support for the U.S. defense strategy of deploying an MRC-scale intervention force into a Eurasian regional crisis.

A secondary but high-priority feature of the conceptual MEII was a set of rules and regulations sponsored by the federal government to encourage the owners and operators of the various national infrastructures to take measures to reduce their infrastructures' vulnerability and/or to ensure rapid reconstitution in the face of IW-type attacks.

Participants' Reactions/Perspectives

The prospect of future major damage to infrastructure in the United States during the course of the crisis was taken very seriously by the exercise participants. Several groups became so concerned about the vulnerability of the United States to further strategic IW-type attacks that they chose very cautious escalation options. Many proponents of this perspective expressed considerable concern about the likely prospect that the United States was more vulnerable to a strategic information warfare campaign than the opponent, in this case Iran. The second school of thought favored some IW response to what was perceived as a sophisticated form of Iranian aggression. Although some members were troubled by the problems and prospects of controlling escalation in this crisis, they strongly believed that a passive approach would set a disastrous precedent by validating IW-type techniques as a new type of warfare.

On the matter of defensive measures for the U.S. infrastructure, there were two schools of thought. Most groups were skeptical about taking any decisive action other than providing reassurance to the American public that the various infrastructures of the United States had a capacity to suffer disruption but could be reconstituted. There was a broad consensus among most groups that dramatic action would "do more harm than good," causing even greater disruption to the particular infrastructure under attack rather than providing a defensive benefit. Most groups favored a cautious public affairs posture with the watchwords, "Don't promise the public too much."

A second school of thought was prepared to recommend to the president that several defensive measures should be taken, including bank and market holidays. This would also provide the federal government the opportunity to show the public that the infrastructure under attack had a capacity to reconstitute within a short period of time.

Several groups were prepared to acknowledge that the scenario presented such an acute dilemma that they would recommend promoting a quick compromise to the political issues within Saudi Arabia if it facilitated an IW deescalation and cease-fire vis-á-vis the U.S. infrastructure. Others rejected this approach and pressured for large-scale IW and/or other conventional weapon counterattacks against Iran.

Several participants noted that the most useful defensive measures were those that the various owners and operators of the various infrastructures could take to reduce vulnerability to attack, heighten vigilance against attack, and provide active procedures for reconstitution. One group decided that whatever the MEII is, it should be used with the understanding that most elements of a response would be procedural rather than the activation of a specific system.

Several teams emphasized that the president should address the country on the potential consequences the public may face as a result of IW actions. It was judged especially important to have the American public see that positive actions were being taken to protect their funds and assets in the financial sector.

Next Steps/Step Three

There was a broad consensus among exercise participants that no dramatic measures, such as shutting down an infrastructure, would be effective as a defensive measure (and some skepticism as to whether such action would, in fact, be possible during a crisis). There appeared, however, to be a broad consensus in favor of exploring the concept of an MEII based on a series of federally sponsored incentives to ensure that the owners and operators have procedures to detect IW-type attacks and reconstitution measures that would minimize the impact of any one network disruption. For reasons of costs and technical feasibility, there was little support for an exclusively federally owned and operated MEII.

It should be noted that the feasibility of achieving an MEII along the lines cited above was greeted with substantial skepticism by some of the exercise participants, largely on the basis that the current dependence on a multitude of systems could not be significantly reduced, even with prior planning. Everyone agreed that there was a need for a rigorous feasibility assessment on the concept.

Figure 12 summarizes the findings for this feature.

RAND *MR661-12*

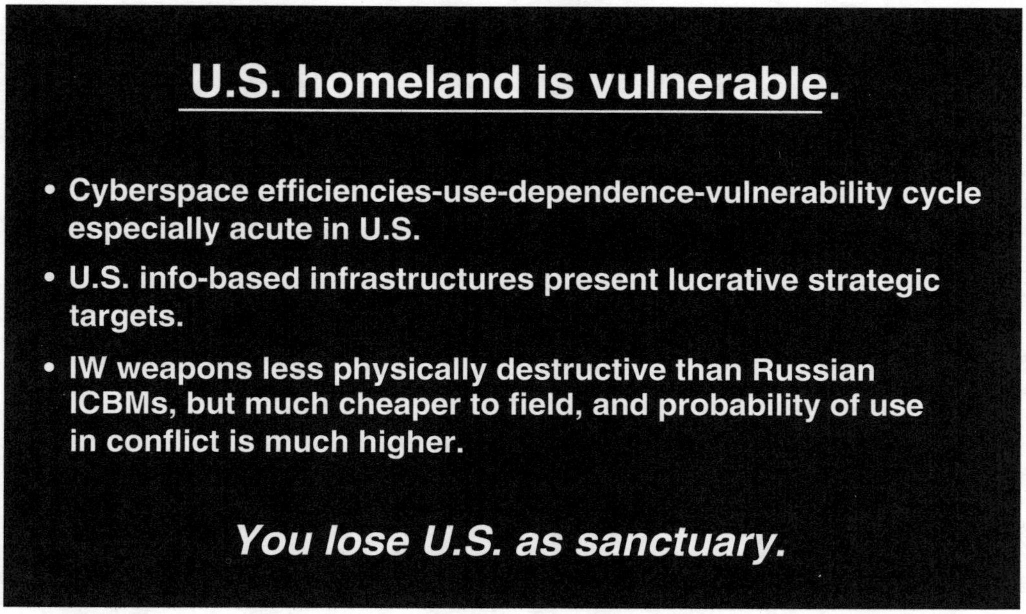

U.S. homeland is vulnerable.

- Cyberspace efficiencies-use-dependence-vulnerability cycle especially acute in U.S.

- U.S. info-based infrastructures present lucrative strategic targets.

- IW weapons less physically destructive than Russian ICBMs, but much cheaper to field, and probability of use in conflict is much higher.

You lose U.S. as sanctuary.

Figure 12—Vulnerability of the U.S. Homeland Summary

Chapter Five

ISSUES OF STRATEGIC INFORMATION WARFARE

Over the course of the exercises, a number of possible issues for near-term consideration and decisionmaking were described. Those addressed in detail below appear to represent both a sound and feasible starting point on this difficult subject. Others that were considered but judged not yet ready for high-level consideration included educational initiatives, development of policy on assistance to allies, the possible establishment of a cyberspace regulatory agency, and military organizational issues.

RISK ASSESSMENT

The issue of whether and how the federal government should conduct a risk assessment of strategic information warfare threats contains within it the basic question of "Risk to what enterprise?"

This question is similar to the frequently asked question concerning "the role of deterrence" in a post–cold war security environment. During the early phases of post–cold war security discussions, there was a tendency to presume that a deterrent posture could impose a "state of being" on a particular regional conflict environment. Over time, however, there developed a wider appreciation of the transitive character of the verb "deter": Who was deterring whom from doing what by what threat of retaliation? In a similar fashion, many discussions about IW risk assessment and strategy frequently take on the vague and unspecified quality of existential deterrence—shown in the uncritical assertion of some national security strategists that "they would not dare."

Through the vehicle of the exercise, many groups were able to address in a much more focused fashion the prospect of conducting an assessment of IW risks to U.S. current national security strategy. There was agreement that, as a minimum, a risk assessment required answers to the question, "How might our current and future capacity to execute the major elements of our national military strategy be compromised or even defeated by new information warfare threats against key elements of the national information infrastructure?"

Such a risk assessment will require an examination of how new information warfare capabilities might be used against a particular target array to defeat a major element of U.S. national military strategy, e.g., the requirement to conduct two nearly simultaneous MRCs. As described in this analysis, there are four potential theaters of military operations—the U.S. homeland or "Zone of the Interior" (ZI), the intercontinental deployment process, the theater battle space, and allied ZI's—which provide a more complete picture of a future conflict environment from the perspective of future IW threats and infrastructure vulnerabilities. Each of these "theaters of operation" is likely to have unique features that will call for different types of risk assessment. Here, as noted, one of the major difficulties in conducting a credible interagency risk assessment is that many of the potential threats and targets cross traditional boundaries between law enforcement and military matters.

Overall, there was a strong consensus among exercise participants that a risk assessment along the above lines should be conducted by the federal government. There was no consensus, however, on how this effort should be organized. One school of thought strongly believed that this assessment could be successfully conducted within the current structure of the U.S. intelligence community. As one advocate of this point of view put it, "What is needed is the right tasking." Others were skeptical about such an approach. Some advocated the creation of a new agency for this and related purposes, which would cut across jurisdictional lines between those agencies responsible for dealing with domestic and foreign security threats. Along these lines, one suggestion was to expand the role of the National Communications System (NCS), giving it broader responsibility to collect and evaluate IW threats and risks.

The general concept of a new federal organization, or one with a greatly expanded mandate, was strongly opposed by two different factions: Some believed that the current environment of federal government retrenchment precluded the creation of a new agency and/or organization even if only as a risk assessment center, while others were strongly opposed to any institutional commingling of the tasks of domestic law enforcement and national intelligence community.

While acknowledging that the creation of a new organization was "premature," there was a school of thought that believed that the risk assessment process (as well as other strategic IW-related matters) should be centralized at a "focal point," or task force leader, of an interagency risk assessment process. Some believed this focal point might reside in either the Office of Management and Budget, the National Security Council, or the Office of the Vice President.

NATIONAL MILITARY STRATEGY

The current national military strategy gives great emphasis to the maintenance of a U.S. capacity to project power on significant scale into key regions of Eurasia—the two nearly simultaneous MRCs as defined by the 1993 DoD Bottom-Up Review (BUR) and subsequent refinements. Further, this strategy posits that the United States will be able to defeat future regional adversaries with forces made smaller by exploiting advances in C3I technologies—i.e., that the United States will be able to gain "dominant battlefield awareness" in future regional conflicts. Also implicit in this strategy is that the United States will be able to project power against a regional adversary that has little or no capacity to threaten the U.S. ZI.

This anticipated exploitation of advanced C3I will, over time, allow the U.S. military to substitute "efficiency for mass"—to deploy strategically agile and efficient forces into future regional theaters of operations over transoceanic distances with far greater logistics efficiency. In the face of projected budget pressures, there are high hopes that much of this new C3I capability can be acquired through a commercial off-the-shelf (COTS) process without incurring any unusual vulnerabilities.

U.S. current national military strategy does not acknowledge the possibility that an opponent will simultaneously attack targets in all four of the cyberspace theaters of operation cited above. Of special concern is the planning assumption that the United States will remain a sanctuary during any future MRC—which is probably obsolescent.

As noted above, there are powerful operational and cost factors that are pushing the U.S. military to exploit the fruits of what has been called the Revolution in Military Affairs (RMA). RMA investments that do not take into account vulnerabilities that might emerge from the evolution of cyberspace could thus set the stage for catastrophic system failures and place the overall national military strategy at risk.

The U.S. battlefield C3I system vulnerabilities to radio-electronic combat may become less significant in the face of U.S. national infrastructure vulnerabilities to cyberspace weapon attacks. As noted, the significance of distance is greatly reduced in IW, and the boundaries between the different theaters of military operation can become blurred. This suggests that future opponents may attempt to bypass U.S. technological and material strength within a potential regional theater of operation and attack strategic vulnerabilities that may reside in the ZI's of the United States or key U.S. allies. In essence, future opponents will exploit cyberspace weapons to "attack U.S. strategy" and not necessarily directly confront U.S. tactical/operational warfighting capability.

These new "strategic" vulnerabilities raise profound questions as to whether and how the USG will be able to devise a credible continental defense against cyberspace weapon attacks. Central to a high-confidence solution to the continental defense problem is the successful conceptual defining and implementing of an MEII as described above, which will allow the United States to continue to project military power on a significant scale in the face of cyberspace weapon attacks. Failure to design and maintain some kind of MEII that is credible in the face of increasingly technologically sophisticated potential opponents will set the stage for future conflicts in which the United States will be readily subjected to strategic IW attacks.

The precise construction of an MEII with its mixture of systems, procedures, laws, and tax incentives remains as an exercise for the future. It is likely that any such attempt to protect the United States from cyberspace weapon attacks will not be leak proof. This raises the question, What is the role of the threat of retaliation to deter attacks? Unlike the development of deterrence strategies during the nuclear weapons revolution, the appearance of a strategic IW threat raises very troubling issues for which a deterrence approach may not be practical. First, there are the major questions, How will one make retaliatory threats and against whom when there is great uncertainty about the origin of an attack. Second, there is the question of the proportionality of any response when the immediate and collateral damage associated with a particular act of cyberspace retaliation is poorly understood by national decisionmakers. Third is the potential asymmetry of vulnerability between the United States, its allies, and the potential opponent. Current contingency plans focus on potential regional adversaries that are technologically less advanced than the United States. The United States may place a far more valuable portion of its national infrastructure at risk than a less-developed country. All of this points to the prospect that there will be no low-cost and conceptually simple deterrent concept that obviates the need to worry about future cyberspace attacks.

NATIONAL SECURITY STRATEGY

Figure 13 shows a spectrum of different kinds of preparedness (but not amounts of preparedness) across the U.S. information infrastructure. On the left is traditional military preparedness with various listed descriptors. The epitome of this kind of preparedness was the Minimum Essential Emergency Communications Network (MEECN), designed to ensure execution of U.S. nuclear war plans. On the right are nonmilitary means of preparedness characterized as shown and exemplified by the new and growing Internet. Incidentally, portions of the MEECN reside on systems found more to the right, like the public switched net; and portions of the Internet may be found in the defense information infrastructure toward the left of this figure.

As one moves from left to right on the spectrum, events resembling war tend to look more like crime, foreign threats look more domestic, government responsibilities fade to private issues, and within government, the federal level changes to the local level.

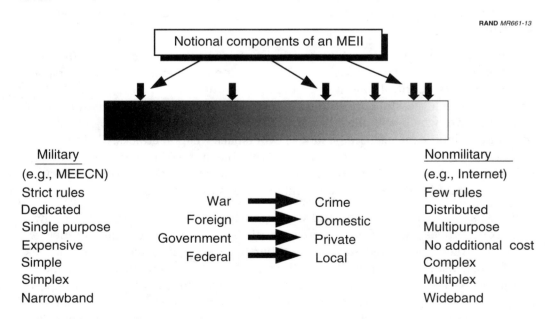

Figure 13—A Spectrum of National Security Preparedness

The concept of an MEII as introduced in the exercise would consist of that minimum portion of various U.S. information infrastructures critical to the functioning of the nation. This fraction of the total NII would be protected from IW attack (albeit in as yet undescribed ways). The participants struggled with this concept, articulating the final consensus with this representative quote: "We don't know what it is, but we must have it."

An actual example of what is being discussed here is the Government Emergency Telecommunications Service, or GETS. This multiagency federal program enables civil, military, and industry officials to use the commercial public telecommunications network in emergencies. GETS is mandated by executive order and administered by the National Communications System with Defense Department funding. It is a software-based approach to preparedness and may represent the beginning of an MEII.

Since it is not feasible to protect the entire U.S. information infrastructure from attack, the vertical arrows along the top of the spectrum represent "point defenses" defined by selecting the parts of the infrastructure most critical to military and civilian operations and then defending them by whatever means appropriate and affordable. For example, the arrow on the far left could indicate a portion of the military infrastructure placed on dedicated fiber optic cables with protected input/output switches procured by the Defense Department to ensure essential point-to-point communications to enhance force deployment capabilities. One of the arrows toward the right could represent a law that would allow cooperation between the intelligence community and domestic law enforcement agencies to improve the gathering of intelligence on U.S. citizens who operate in cyberspace counter to U.S. national interests—or that would impose some protection standards. The arrow on the far right could be a tax incentive that would encourage commercial firms to cooperate with U.S government–led protection processes and to develop reconstitution capabilities.

U.S. GOVERNMENT ROLE

Figure 14 portrays a spectrum of existing and potential governmental roles across military and nonmilitary issues. It is clear that the role that the federal government will play in all of this is fundamental; this assertion cropped up throughout the exercise series. However, as we move from constitutional requirements for national defense through public safety toward things that represent the public good, the role of government changes. The operative emphasis of governing changes from operation to facilitation—from owning fiber optic cables to enacting tax incentives. Clearly, the government's perceived role in this area will have to be balanced against public perceptions of the loss of civil liberties and the commercial sector's concern about unwarranted limits on its practices and markets.

As in any new issue of potential government involvement in an area with strong domestic economic and social equities, the extent and character of the government role is certain to stimulate strong debate. In this context, participants seem to prefer that government and industry act cooperatively in pursuit of their interrelated goals.

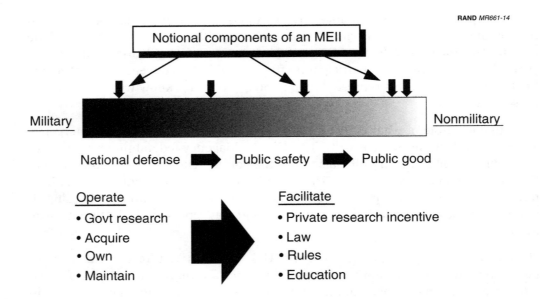

Figure 14—A Spectrum of U.S. Government Roles

The extensive participation of industry in the exercises was highly encouraging in this regard. A strong government role—in fact, strong government leadership—appeared to be a consensus approach among the great majority of exercise participants. Here again the question cited above of who should be in charge within the executive branch is particularly relevant.

Chapter Six

CONCLUSIONS

The features and likely consequences of strategic information warfare point to a basic conclusion: Key national military strategy assumptions are obsolescent and inadequate for confronting the threat posed by strategic IW. Five major recommendations emerged from the exercises as starting points for addressing this shortcoming. They are discussed below.

LEADERSHIP: WHO SHOULD BE IN CHARGE?

Participants widely agreed that an immediate first step is the assignment of a focal point for federal government leadership toward a coordinated U.S. response to the strategic IW threat. This focal point should be located in the Executive Office of the President, since only at this level can the necessary interagency coordination of the large number of government organizations involved in such matters—and the necessary interactions with the Congress—be effectively carried out. This office should also have the responsibility for close coordination with industry since the nation's information infrastructure is being developed almost exclusively by the commercial sector. Once established, this high-level leadership should, perhaps via a presidential review directive, initiate a comprehensive review of national-level information warfare issues.

RISK ASSESSMENT

The federal government leadership entity cited above should, as a first step, conduct an immediate risk assessment to determine, to the degree possible, the extent of the vulnerability of key elements of current U.S. national security and national military strategy to strategic information warfare. Strategic target sets, IW weapons effects, and parallel vulnerability and threat assessments should be among the components of this review. In an environment of dynamic change in both cyberspace threats and vulnerabilities, there is no sound basis for presidential decisionmaking on strategic IW matters without such a risk assessment.

In this context, there is always the hope or the belief—we saw both in the exercises—that the kind of aggressive response suggested in this report can be delayed while cyberspace gets a chance to evolve robust defenses on its own. This is, in fact, a possibility—that the healing and annealing of an immune system that is under constant assault, as cyberspace is and assuredly will continue to be (if only, in Willy Sutton's words, because that's where the money is), will create the robust NII that everyone hopes to use. But it may not, and we are certainly not there now.

Against this difficult projection and assessment situation, there is the ever-present risk that the United States could find itself in a crisis in the near term, facing the possibility of, or indications of, a strategic IW attack. When the president asks whether the United States is under IW attack—and, if so, by whom—and whether the U.S. military plan and strategy are vulnerable, "We do not have the foggiest idea" will not be an acceptable answer.

GOVERNMENT'S ROLE

The appropriate role for government in responding to the strategic IW threat needs to be addressed, with the recognition that this role—part leadership and part partnership with the domestic sector—is certain to evolve. In addition to performing certain basic preparedness functions—such as organizing, equipping, training, and sustaining military forces—the government could play a more productive and efficient role as facilitator and maintainer of some information systems and infrastructure, and—through policy mechanisms such as tax breaks—could encourage reducing vulnerability and improving recovery and reconstitution capability.

NATIONAL SECURITY STRATEGY

Once an initial risk assessment has been completed, preparedness for the threat as identified needs to be appropriately addressed in U.S. national security strategy. Preparedness for IW will cross several traditional boundaries across the spectrum from "military" to "civilian," from "foreign" to "domestic," and from "national" to "local."

One promising means for instituting this kind of preparedness could involve the concept of a minimum essential information infrastructure. The MEII is conceived as the minimum portion of various U.S. information systems critical to ensure the nation's continued functioning. An assessment of the feasibility of an MEII should be made.

NATIONAL MILITARY STRATEGY

The current national military strategy emphasizes maintaining U.S. capability to project power into theaters of operation in key regions of Europe and Asia. There are four emerging theaters of operation in cyberspace: the theater battlefield, the transoceanic lines of communication, allied states' Zones of Interior, and the U.S. Zone of Interior. Strategic IW reduces the significance of distance with respect to the deployment and use of weapons. Therefore, battlefield C3I vulnerabilities may become less significant than vulnerabilities in the national infrastructure. Consideration of these IW features should be accounted for in U.S. national military strategy.

ADDITIONAL READING: THREATS AND VULNERABILITIES

Below is a partial listing of references that we used in the scenario design. This material provides additional perspective on the current state of experience and thinking regarding most of the strategic information warfare threats and vulnerabilities addressed in this study.

Arquilla, John, and David Ronfeldt. "Cyberwar is Coming!" *Comparative Strategy*, Vol. 12, 1993, pp. 141-165.

Defense Science Board Summer Study Task Force. "Appendix B: Information Warfare." *Report on Information Architecture for the Battlefield.* October, 1994.

Richard O. Hundley and Robert H. Anderson, "Emerging Challenge: Security and Safety in Cyberspace," in *IEEE Technology and Society Magazine* (Special Issue on Computers and Society), forthcoming.

Richard O. Hundley and Robert H. Anderson, *Security in Cyberspace: An Emerging Challenge for Society*, RAND, P-7893, December 1994.

Joint Security Commission. "Chapter 8: Information Systems Security." *Redefining Security.* Government Printing Office, Washington, D.C.; 1994.

Libicki, Martin. "What Is Information Warfare?" *Strategic Forum.* Institute for National Strategic Studies, National Defense University; Number 28; May 1995.

National Communications System. *The Electronic Intrusion Threat to National Security and Emergency Preparedness Telecommunications.* Office of the Manager, NCS; Arlington, VA; December 5, 1994.

National Research Council. *Computers at Risk: Safe Computing in the Information Age.* National Academy Press, Washington, D.C.; 1991.

Neumann, Peter. *Computer Related Risks.* Addison-Wesley, New York; 1995.

Raymond, Eric, ed. *The On-Line Hacker Jargon File.* Version 2.9.10; July 1992.

Stoll, Clifford. *The Cuckoo's Egg.* Pocket Books, Simon and Schuster, New York; 1989.

————. "Defence Technology: The Information Advantage." *The Economist.* June 10, 1995.

————. "Police, FBI Hunt for Hacker Who Upset Internet Service." *The Seattle Times.* July 12, 1995.

METHODOLOGY

The "Day After . . ." methodology[1] of the exercises employed in this study involves a three-step half-day process (see Figure A.1) in which participants take on the role of top advisors to a national decisionmaker (e.g., the U.S. president) in a group deliberative process akin to a classic time-constrained "pre-meeting" in advance of a formal deliberative/decisionmaking meeting (e.g., in advance of a U.S. National Security Council Meeting).

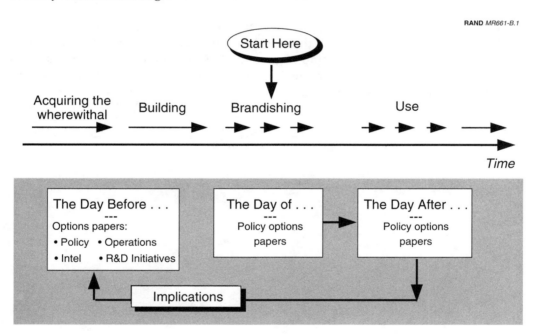

Figure A.1—The "Day After . . ." Exercise Methodology

---

[1]For examples of previous uses of this methodology to explore the national security implications of the continued diffusion of nuclear weapons capabilities see (1) Millot, Molander, and Wilson, "The Day After . . . Study: Nuclear Proliferation in the Post–Cold War World," Volumes I-III, 1993 (RAND MR-266-AF, MR-253-AF, MR-267-AF) and (2) Mesic, Molander, and Wilson, "Strategic Futures: Evolving Missions for Traditional Strategic Delivery Vehicles," 1995 (RAND MR-375-DAG).

The process begins (Step One) with the group (nominally 8 to 10 people under a chairman) addressing the critical issues that are manifest on "*the day of*" a pivotal change in the political-military status quo in some crisis context. In this step, there is invariably an explicit or implicit brandishing of "strategic weapons" of some character (strategic information options in the exercise developed in this study).

Second, the exercise turns to "*the day after*" (Step Two)—the aftermath of actual strategic weapon "use" of some kind (in this case the aggressive use of a variety of strategic information options)—and explores a new set of crisis-driven choices.

Finally, the exercise moves to "*the day before*" (Step Three)—in the present or near future, considering the challenge of devising and marketing new initiatives (policies or strategies, operational concepts, weapons R&D initiatives, or intelligence initiatives) to help minimize the prospect that a strategic crisis like the one just faced could occur—or, if it did occur, to mitigate the consequences and reduce the likelihood that it would ever occur again. This third step of the exercise is designed to draw out participants on an action agenda, while the problems encountered in the first two steps are still in the forefront of their minds—as in Samuel Johnson's famous aphorism, "The threat of hanging concentrates the mind."

In all the steps (usually, two or three different groups do the exercise simultaneously and compare results after each of the steps), the group's task is to revise a draft of a concise "issues and options" memo (e.g., to the U.S. president) on the key issues to be taken up at the imminent deliberative/decisionmaking meeting—and, where possible, to forge consensus on recommendations on individual issues.

SUMMARY OF GROUP DELIBERATIONS FOR STEP THREE

OVERVIEW

The material that follows summarizes the responses of the exercise participants to the policy issues raised in Step Three during the June 3 version of "The Day After . . . in Cyberspace." See Figures B.1 and B.2, which provide an outline of the flow in decisionmaking by the seven groups during Step One and Step Two of the exercise.

Team A

Team A felt TW/AA and risk assessment need to be done in parallel. The group believed that it was very important to understand the vulnerability of national systems when carrying out this risk assessment. Out of this, an overall national intelligence estimate (NIE) should evolve. The group believed there is a lot of work to be completed on foreign and domestic intelligence cooperation, which may require changes in the law to facilitate foreign intelligence and domestic law enforcement cooperation. The group observed that there is no policy in place to develop a doctrine and a resulting strategy for both offensive and defensive IW. When such a doctrine is in place, the strategy should be a living document because of the rapid changes in information technology. A new independent federal entity, perhaps called the national information officer, reporting to the vice president should be created. This individual could access all "relevant" federal agencies throughout the government in a matrix fashion. Members of Team A thought that the approach might be similar to the way the continuity-of-government issue was handled about 10 years ago.

Team B

Team B felt that it would be harder to address near-term issues than some of the longer-term ones. This group also thought that a leader must be chosen at the level of the Executive Office of the President. There was a consensus that this individual should be within the Office of Management and Budget (OMB) and that OMB could provide the necessary interaction across all agencies of government. There was a strong consensus within Team B that there is a particular need to have good

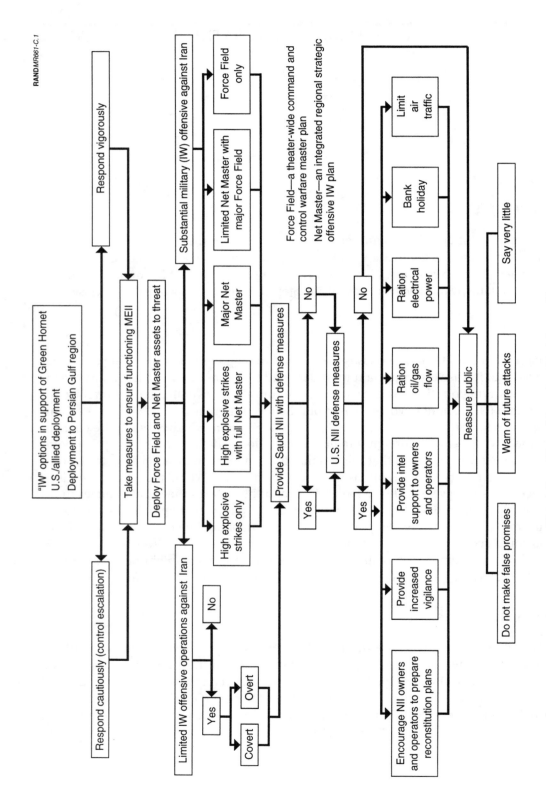

Figure B.1—Flow of Step One Decisionmaking

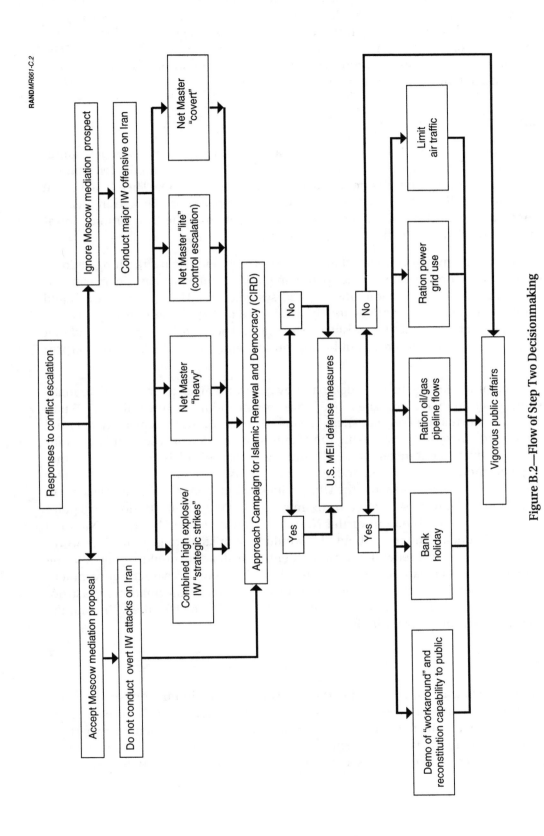

Figure B.2—Flow of Step Two Decisionmaking

cooperation between the intelligence community and the Department of Justice. This group felt that an MEII is neither feasible nor affordable, and that its elements are neither well understood. If an MEII is to be developed, they felt that some combination of the National Communications System/National Security Tele-communications Advisory Committee (NCS/NSTAC) should be responsible for it with OMB again providing the focal point.

Team C

The consensus of Team C was that the federal government should take a less ambitious role in protecting the national infrastructure. Team C members felt that the vulnerability of cyberspace is not an all-or-nothing proposition. They believe that the country can live with some vulnerabilities. Cyberspace has many strengths, and we need to exploit these strengths to provide protection to the U.S. national infra-structure. One such strength is its highly distributed nature.

There are too many actors involved in cyberspace to develop an overarching national strategy. Those organizations that operate in global cyberspace have increasing incentives to reduce the vulnerabilities of their systems. The U.S. government should exploit these natural incentives for the providers and end users to improve the overall national infrastructure's resilience to attack. Therefore, this group found that strong government action may not be appropriate and may, in fact, be counterproductive.

They recommended the use of a deft hand by government so actors can try to make systems safer on their own. The role of government should be threefold: (1) to participate in information consciousness-raising, (2) to coordinate some activities, and (3) to provide incentives for making the overall system safer. These could be tax incentives or investment incentives, etc. However, members of Team C believed that the government needs to respond to threats of IW with military actions where needed. The consensus was that the United States should be prepared to use force to defend U.S. vital interests. Team C recommended that the administration focal point should be some combination of the National Security Council and the National Economic Council. The team thought it would be a mistake to give the TW/AA responsibility to a single federal government entity; instead it should be given to the NCS/NSTAC. With regard to the MEII, the group felt that in this case the government could not depend on the marketplace to provide a national information infrastructure that would be resilient to IW-type attacks. There is a need for the MEII, and the DoD is the appropriate place for it.

Team D

Team D concentrated on examining the issues that lay behind the questions. They felt there was a critical need for risk assessments and there is much to be learned about the vulnerability of the national information infrastructure. The mere perception of a vulnerability may represent a very large strategic threat. The real issue is that "cyberspace vulnerability" is a technology/policy problem and that some of the political problems will perhaps be hardest to resolve. Members of Team D expressed concern about the conflict between public and general privacy laws. They recommended that these issues be debated in Congress as a means of generating awareness and identifying paths toward consensus solutions, perhaps to offer different approaches for their solution. These might be (1) a voluntary approach—between government and industry—or (2) a regulatory approach. As to the question of who should be in charge, this group felt it should be someone just below the president.

Team E

Team E felt it was very important to articulate goals and strategies first, before laying out a management approach. The consensus of the group pointed to a need for a risk assessment, but the responsibility for this assessment should be distributed throughout all relevant agencies of the government. The group members believed that one organization could aggregate all of these different agency inputs and provide it to a coordinating official in the Executive Office of the President. They suggested an expanded NCS combined with a civil agency to be responsible for the risk and threat information. The group consensus was that the National Security Agency (NSA) clearly has the best ability to monitor the civilian infrastructure to determine the threat. Several members of the team questioned whether the country was willing to allow NSA to take on this responsibility. This group felt it is very important to have a long-term reevaluation of how a new NCS may be chartered given the new challenges.

Team F

Team F felt it was very difficult to develop solutions to the postulated vulnerability of the information infrastructure. Instead they examined a framework to think about the problem. They believed that this framework should include an assessment of such issues as (1) deterrence—deter by the spectrum of instruments that you can apply or deter by denial (from the information attack or from conventional attack); (2) cost pressures—there are extreme pressures to reduce the costs of operating the national information infrastructure, and thus companies do not put funds into protecting these systems. However, the infrastructure is very diverse and therefore provides inherent protection. Several members of Team F emphasized the issue of "asymmetrical vulnerabilities." The United States relies heavily on information systems to operate its national infrastructure, but many U.S. adversaries do not. Therefore, Team F believed that the United States faces a severe asymmetrical threat.

Team G

Team G reached concensus that it is very important to create a typology of major IW issues. The team believed that there is a need to understand what deterrence and escalation control/dominance means in this context. As for organizational issues, this group felt it was very important to develop a pool of resources that can deal with this type of problem. Team G felt that a task force or commission might be the best approach. They acknowledged the need for intellectual leadership (thinkers during the early nuclear era such as Kahn and Brodie were cited as examples) and agreed that there was a need to bring extraordinary intellectual resources to bear on this problem. Several members of Team G felt that there also needs to be a "sunset clause" to many federal initiatives dealing with informational infrastructure so that each one does not carry on forever. This group also felt it was very important to think of the problem as an international one and not just in terms of U.S. vulnerabilities.

EXERCISE

Appendix C provides a complete reprint of "The Day After . . . in Cyberspace" exercise held at the National Defense University on June 3, 1995.

The Day After...

...in Cyberspace

The "Day After..." methodology requires a realistic scenario; however, specific companies, systems, or system components appearing in this scenario are examples only and their appearance implies no unique capability or vulnerability. Attribution to any organization or entity shall not be made as a result of the text contained herein.

STEP ONE

RAND

3 June 1995

TABLE OF CONTENTS

The Day After...

...in Cyberspace

Roger C. Molander
Peter A. Wilson
Andrew S. Riddile
Robert H. Anderson
John Arquilla
Steven C. Bankes
Anthony C. Hearn
Richard O. Hundley
Richard F. Mesic
Kevin O'Connell
David F. Ronfeldt

METHODOLOGY

"The Day After..." exercise methodology has been developed to explore and assess evolving post-Cold War strategic problems in the area of national security. The exercise design is based on a three step process lasting a total of approximately four hours. Participants take on the role of top advisors to a national decision-maker (e.g., the U.S. President) or a decision-making body (e.g., NATO) in a group deliberative process akin to a classic time-constrained "pre-meeting" in advance of a formal deliberative/ decision-making meeting (e.g., a "principals plus one" meeting in advance of a U.S. National Security Council Meeting).

The process begins (see schematic below) with the group convened to examine the critical issues that are manifest on "the day of" (STEP ONE)--a change or foreshadowed change in the strategic status quo in some future crisis context.

As a second pivotal point, the exercise turns to "the day after" (STEP TWO)--the aftermath of a major strategic event at a later point in the same crisis context (e.g., nuclear weapon use or strategic information warfare attack)--and explores a new set of crisis-driven choices.

As a final decision point, the exercise moves to "the day before" (STEP THREE)--to the present or near future--and considers the challenges in _one or more_ of the elements of:

(1) crafting new strategies and/or policies,

(2) creating new institutional structures,

(3) designing new operational concepts,

(4) launching new R&D initiatives, or

(5) launching new intelligence initiatives

to help minimize the prospect that crises such as that just faced would occur--or, if they do, to mitigate their consequences, and reduce the likelihood that they would ever occur again.

In all of the steps the group's task is to revise a draft of an "issues and options" memo on the key issues to be taken up at the imminent deliberative/ decision-making meeting--and, where possible, to forge consensus on recommendations on individual issues.

In general, two or more groups go through the identical exercise at the same time and compare results and recommendations at the end of each step.

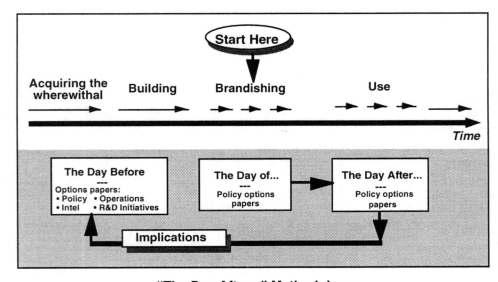

"The Day After..." Methodology
(Examples: Facing Regional Adversaries with Nuclear Weapons or
Strategic Information Warfare Capability)

STEP ONE: The Day Of...

SITUATION REPORT

BACKGROUND

It is now mid-spring in **the year 2000.**

As the Twentieth Century drew to a close, **political changes and continued unrest** in the **Persian Gulf**, in **Pakistan**, in the **Islamic countries of the former Soviet Union**, and across the breadth of **North Africa** had created a new and profoundly troubled region of the world now frequently labeled **"the Islamic Arc of Crisis."**

Adding to U.S. and European concerns about this region was the rising prospect that one or more of the **potential predators** in the region had developed the capacity to **exploit the Global Information Infrastructure (GII) as a field of strategic political-military operations.**

The latter situation has sparked particular **anxiety** in the U.S. about the **safety and security** of **the U.S. National Information Infrastructure (NII)** and **an evolving Defense Information Infrastructure (DII)** (see below).

MAJOR FEATURES OF THE GII, NII, AND DII

In the 1990s the **Cellular Revolution** proceeded apace with the availability of new low and medium earth orbit satellite constellations such as *Iridium* and *Globestar* providing **readily accessible global two-way communications via portable telephones.** It is now estimated that 25% of the North American, European, and Japanese adults routinely carry a cellphone. A similar explosion of cellphone use continues in other major markets.

The Internet has become a pillar of both the NII and GII. All countries now have Internet hosts, and it is estimated that 70% of the world's population now lives within a local telephone call of an Internet gateway.

The phenomenon of **the World Wide Web has continued to expand, with over one million "home pages" of information** providing links to data bases around the world. Many of these home pages include video and voice releases specially designed for consumption by the mass media.

One of the most significant trends of the past decade has been the **growth of electronic commerce.** Current estimates suggest that **a third of all formal U.S. business transactions now occur electronically** using both standardized data interchanges and specialized communications between cooperating companies employing a range of digital encryption standards. **Attempts by the U.S. government to establish a hardware encryption standard** (successors to the CLIPPER CHIP initiative) **have been thwarted** by lawsuits brought by both citizen groups and software companies.

The NII and GII are also being heavily used by a **new generation of activist groups.** Many such groups are **linked in transnational networks** that address a broad range of environmental, human-rights, and other global issues.

The **Internet** and **World Wide Web** have become **virtual battlegrounds for software "user agents" of various types.** Tens of thousands of such agents have been unleashed to roam "the NET" and "the WEB" looking for items meeting a profile of interests of their users. Other agents spend their time blocking access to information deemed private or sensitive, and scanning individual systems for viruses, worms and other "beasties" inhabiting cyberspace.

In 1998 the President decided to allow **the bulk of the Defense Department's "peacetime and administrative communications"** to continue to **rely on the commercial switched telephone and public data systems.** The vast majority of DII communications now pass over the commercial **Public Switched Network (PSN)**, relying on **various levels of encryption** to protect classified information.

During the period from 1995-2000 **various largely unsuccessful attempts** were made **to increase the security of the PSN.** These efforts have been complicated by the fact that **"the PSN" is run and maintained by many competing companies** including cable, cellular, and satellite operators, so that changes are difficult to mandate and place into effect. As a result, other than individual use of end-to-end encryption by cooperating parties, **PSN security in the year 2000 is not much better than that in 1995.**

SITUATION REPORT (cont.)

As the result of the now famous Black Widow virus attack on MCI's PSN in June 1997, **a Minimum Essential Information Infrastructure (MEII)**--so-called "emergency lanes on the information highway"--was established in 1999 to meet the criterion of being able to support "deployment and wartime operations for two nearly simultaneous Major Regional Contingencies (MRCs)."

The resilience of the MEII against a possible adversary information warfare (IW) campaigns has recently become subject to question--a legacy of several near-successes in MEII penetration efforts by unknown parties.

In light of the above environment, in the last few years there has been **rising concern over the increasing interdependence** of the PSN, the U.S. electrical power grid, data networks supporting the air traffic control system, the Global Positioning Satellites (GPS) system, and other key U.S. infrastructure elements. As a result both national security and law enforcement agencies in the U.S. (and in other nations) are devoting **increasing resources to assessing and countering both domestic and foreign IW threats.**

MAJOR FEATURES OF THE GLOBAL SECURITY ENVIRONMENT

Saudi Arabia Under Stress

The past few years have seen **major steps by the Saudi government to open up Saudi society politically, economically, and socially.** New independent television stations are now broadcasting and there has been wide proliferation of direct broadcast satellite receivers and cellular telecommunications systems. All elements of society are making increasing use of a variety of Internet nodes.

The **Saudi monarchy has suffered substantially** from internal dissent and distress since the 1997 death of King Fahd. **A weak successor now struggles to govern both the family and the kingdom,** which is increasingly beset by **growing tensions between an Islamic fundamentalist dissident movement and the "nationalist modernizers"** who currently dominate the Saudi government.

By 1998, much of the **Saudi dissident movement** (especially within the universities) had **coalesced around the goals and objectives of the increasingly influential Campaign for Islamic Renewal and Democracy (CIRD).** This loose transnational CIRD coalition, formed at the 1997 Damascus meeting of Islamic state and non-governmental organizations (NGOs), has become **a prominent force for social and political change** in the **Persian Gulf** region as well as **throughout the Islamic world.**

The CIRD is **very well funded**, principally by North American and European Islamic sources but also in part by domestic sources in Saudi Arabia, Iran, and Pakistan. The **CIRD exploits a variety of modern advanced information and communications technologies** for organizing, fund-raising, media coverage, and building ties to organizations throughout the global Islamic and broader NGO community. Several CIRD chapters are now very **prominent within the North American Islamic community.**

Oil prices have remained stable throughout the 1990s which has forced the Saudi Kingdom to make **cutbacks in ambitious domestic and social programs** designed in part to "keep domestic peace."

Adding to the Saudi kingdom's fiscal woes is the broad **consensus within the monarchy and government elites**--strongly opposed by CIRD supporters within Saudi Arabia--that **defense spending must remain high in the face of the increasing military and political power of Iran** (see below).

The Saudi regime's **nervousness about their overall security and financial vulnerability** markedly increased in early 1998 following the revelation that **the Bank of Saudi Arabia had been "looted" of nearly $1.2 billion by a sophisticated electronic attack** which for two months had successfully used "skimming" and other "cyberspace bank robbery" techniques before detection by a British financial security service. The Saudi government later found **strong evidence of both Iranian and Syrian involvement** in the attack.

SITUATION REPORT (cont.)

Persia Ascendant

Iran's power and influence in the Persian Gulf rose dramatically following the **1997 Iraqi civil war** that erupted in the wake of Saddam Hussein's abrupt departure. As a result of a highly effective Iranian intervention in the civil war, **Iraq is now essentially divided.** A weak post-Baathist central government has been installed in Baghdad while the Kurds in the north and Shiites in the south enjoy virtual autonomy in most matters.

Iran openly supports radical Islamic fundamentalist groups in almost all of the Gulf states and trumpets a "pan-Islamic" strategy of building a broad political-military coalition to "resist American and European hegemony in the Islamic world."

Iran's nuclear weapons ambitions are widely acknowledged though there is at present **no evidence that the Iranians have any operational nuclear weapons**. The Iranians continue to maintain that their rapidly growing nuclear infrastructure--which remains under IAEA inspection--is for "nuclear energy alone."

There is some **evidence of a covert Iranian indigenous nuclear weapons program**. Of greater concern are reports that Iran may have been able to **acquire significant quantities of weapons grade highly enriched uranium (HEU) from Russian organized crime sources** in the late-1990s.

Iran continues to improve its long-range weapons delivery capability which currently includes: (1) 36 **Russian Tu-22M Backfires,** (2) an IRBM force of two dozen **North Korean *Nodong II* missiles,** and (3) an MRBM force of 200-300 *Nodong I* **missiles.**

Evidence of the extent of development of Iranian IW activity emerged in 1999 in India when three Indian nationals (including an acknowledged "world class" software writer) were arrested by authorities after penetrating supposedly highly secure Indian defense networks, and in the course of plea-bargaining **confessed to selling Iran "a variety of 21st Century information warfare tools."**

Iran maintains **an uneasy relationship with the CIRD** which has resisted Iranian efforts to convert the coalition to a more fundamentalist Islamic posture. In addition, a number of **CIRD leaders have privately criticized the slow pace of democratization in Iran.** However, intelligence sources report that Iran is channeling funds to some factions within the CIRD coalition.

Algeria

Popular support for the Algerian military martial law government continued to unravel into 1996, and **in April 1996 a pro-Islamic "colonels' faction" led a coup which took control of the government** in concert with the "Rome coalition" of former government opposition groups. In the fall of 1996, an Islamic government was formally established in a new round of national elections.

In the summer of 1998, relations between Algeria and the U.S. and Europe began to deteriorate as the **new Algerian regime increasingly tilted toward the geo-strategic and political interests of Iran** and military cooperation programs between the two countries became more widespread.

During the summer of 1999, French intelligence services were alerted to the **attempted placement of a lethal "polymorphic" computer virus in the latest variant of the AirBus Industries AB-330 flight control software,** apparently by **Algerian agents in France acting under the direction of Iran.** French aviation authorities found that Aerospatiale had been relying upon several Indian software subcontractors which had access to supposedly "secure" source code development and compilers.

Libya

In November of 1998 while flying to inspect a new chemical weapon facility in southern Libya, **President Qadhafi was severely injured** in a helicopter crash and shortly thereafter retired. In the political turmoil that followed, **a strongly nationalist Islamic government quickly seized power** and consolidated control of the country.

Much to the surprise of many observers, the new Libyan government **moved rapidly to hold elections** and embrace "Islamic democracy." It is now viewed as **one of the CIRD's strongest government supporters** in the effort to build a united democracy-based Islamic political force.

SITUATION REPORT (cont.)

Pakistan

In 1997, the **Bhutto regime was overthrown by a military coup** which faulted the government for "political indecisiveness and inadequate military assistance" in the failed "Tet-like" **general uprising in Kashmir in late 1996.**

With the departure of the Bhutto regime, the military-dominated government took on **an increasingly militant Islamic stance** which included **dramatically expanded political-military ties with Iran.**

Israel and the Arabs

Israel signed **peace agreements with both Syria and Lebanon in 1997.**

In the summer of 1999, the Israeli government began to be subject to (in Mossad's terminology) "a new form of strategic warfare"--a series of **electronic attacks on Israel's military command and control system** by a sophisticated array of **"sniffers" and "logic bombs" of uncertain origin.**

The Russian Federation

A strongly "Russian nationalist" regime came to power in the 1996 elections and moved quickly to consolidate power and influence both within the Federation and in "the near abroad."

In 1997 the Russian military created **a new Radio Electronic Combat Command** which has been charged with the development of "a comprehensive 21st Century offensive and defensive information warfare capability."

The new Russian information warfare effort in part reflected acknowledgment of a continuing domestic problem--**increasingly sophisticated internal "cyberspace banditry" techniques employed by Russian "mafiya" organized crime groups.** While such attacks within Russia have diminished, the groups continue to mount successful attacks on European and American banks (with an estimated gain of over $2 billion in the year 1999 alone). U.S. and European intelligence and law enforcement services strongly suspect that **some of the best Russian "mafiya hacker talent" is now in the pay of the Russian intelligence services.**

China

A "tough, pragmatic, and strongly nationalist" leadership has consolidated power in a post-Deng Xiaopeng China which continues to lead Asia on an upward trajectory of economic growth.

Reflecting ever-increasing Chinese self-confidence, there is now a dominant view among the Chinese political and military leadership **that China should acquire "strategic military power second to none" in the early 21st Century.**

A **new and widely remarked Chinese "21st Century strategic asset"** is the acknowledged skill of a emerging generation of **Chinese computer experts** which provide both the Chinese commercial and banking sectors and the government **with world-class offensive and defensive IW "hacker" capability.**

Japan

The Japanese government **interest in potential IW threats** was profoundly **heightened after the "Great Yen crisis of 1998"** when the Japanese currency nearly collapsed after a two-day fall of 22%. Only several months after the fact was there sufficient suspicion the massive fall in the Yen had been partially **"induced by a very sophisticated computer 'Trojan Horse' program"** of which the authors were believed to be an alliance of several **Chinese and other Asian Transnational Criminal Organizations (TCOs).**

The Koreas

Kim Jong Il continues to maintain control over the key levers of power in the DPRK although there continue to be internal power struggles around him between various factions in the North Korean elite--which continues to hold back reunification efforts.

Implementation of the 1994 U.S.-DPRK nuclear "framework" has proceeded in fits and starts, but it continues to be seen as **successful in holding back the North Korean nuclear program.** However, the DPRK maintains a robust indigenous missile development and production program and **an extensive missile export and cooperative development program with Iran.**

SITUATION REPORT (cont.)

The United States

Following the **highly contentious 1996 elections**, there emerged a tentative political consensus that the United States had **no choice but to remain heavily engaged in maintaining a semblance of "international law and order."** At the same time continued public **concerns about acute U.S. domestic problems** appeared to **weigh heavily against seeking costly military solutions** to the evolving menu of security problems.

In this challenging political context there emerged in 1997 **the Consortium for Planetary Peace (CPP),** an unusual grass roots **political coalition with support from both the left and right** and organized around the twin propositions that: (1) it was **not in the U.S. national interest to become "a global policeman"** and (2) **"modern conflict resolution and communications methods" should be aggressively employed** as flagship elements of U.S. international security policy.

With support from a broad range of existing peace, human-rights, environmental, and other activist groups, the CPP grew quickly with a **"start in your own international neighborhood" organizing theme**--using the Internet to organize a wide range of U.S., Canadian, and Mexican NGOs to **focus a coordinated effort on the continued acute political unrest in southern Mexico.** In late 1998 the organization gained considerable prestige by facilitating a widely hailed "peace agreement" between the Mexican government and the "Third Zapatista Revolution."

Building on the success in Mexico, the CPP over the past year and a half has become **increasingly involved as a mediator and Internet organizer of "peacemaking coalitions" in a number of regional and other conflicts around the world** (in which capacity it has developed substantial informal ties with the Islamic CIRD coalition).

In 1998 the **charter of the National Security Telecommunications Advisory Committee (NSTAC)** was expanded from telecommunications matters **to include all national security information system issues.** A **Network Security Steering Committee (NSSC)** established within the NSTAC was given the responsibility of choosing those **elements of the NII to be included in the initial "two MRC" MEII** with a continuing responsibility for **assessing MEII vulnerability.**

A parallel organization created at the same time within the JCS oversees the **development of offensive and defensive operational concepts and campaigns and new requirements for "electronic weapons."** This organization works with the various unified commands to develop Radio Electronic Combat or IW planning annexes for the CINCs' CONPLANs for various contingencies.

Increasing concerns about the viability of the nuclear non-proliferation regime led in 1998 to **major revisions in U.S. force structure plans to make room for a package of counter-proliferation initiatives** which included: (1) A crash effort on the **Theater High Altitude Air Defense (THAAD)** system, (2) Extensive overseas sales of **Patriot/ERINT** and *Standard* anti-tactical missiles, and (3) Accelerated development of **long-endurance unmanned air vehicles (UAVs)** and a companion program of multi-mission **unattended ground sensors (UGS).**

In late 1999 in the wake of the French AirBus incident **U.S. commercial aircraft companies initiated a survey of the software in the flight control systems of aircraft under development** to insure software system integrity. Other than some minor software code errors, nothing was found--but there emerged a heightened vigilance in the commercial aircraft sector to protect these systems.

Persian Gulf Security

In 1999 in the face of Iran's growing political military power, the **U.S., France, and the U.K. updated their military agreements with the Gulf Coordinating Council (GCC).**

The military contingency plans for the region now include the **prepositioning of substantial additional military equipment in the region** and **rapid deployment commitments** code-named **GREEN HORNET** for the U.S. (see Table 1) and **SILVER SABRE** for the U.K. and France.

A British air mobile/motorized and a French air mobile/motorized division along with several squadrons of tactical fighter aircraft constitute the principal European military components of **SILVER SABRE.**

SITUATION REPORT (cont.)

Table 1. Major Components of GREEN HORNET

	Phase One Deterrent Phase	Phase Two Initial Defense	Phase Three Full Capability
Army	• Deploy 2 THAAD battalions • Place 3 Phase Two Divisions on Alert • Deploy Army equipment set from Diego Garcia	• Fully deploy 3 Phase Two Divisions • Place 4 Phase Three Divisions (3 CONUS/1 Europe) on Alert	• Fully deploy 4 Phase Three Divisions • Reserve call-up
Navy	• Move 1 Carrier Battle Group (CBG) to Gulf of Oman • Move 1 *Aegis* to Persian Gulf	• Deploy CBG to Red Sea • Move 1 *Aegis* to Persian Gulf • Move 2 *Aegis* to Med • Partial Ready Reserve Fleet (RRF) call-up	• Deploy 3 CBGs • Move 6 *Aegis* to Theater • Reserve call-up • Full RRF
Air Force	• Deploy 1 Air Combat Wing (ACW) • Deploy AWACS, JSTARS, intel aircraft	• Deploy 3 ACWs	• Deploy 7 ACWs
Marine Corps	• Deploy 1 Maritime Prepositioning Squadron (MPS) from Diego Garcia • Off load in-Theater MPS • Airlift associated CONUS brigade personnel to theater	• Deploy 2 MPS from Atlantic and Pacific • Marry up 2 CONUS brigades w/in-theater MPS equipment • Deploy 2 amphibious brigades from CONUS	• 2 amphibious brigades in Theater • Reserve call-up
Time to Complete	7 Days	21 Days	60 Days

SITUATION REPORT (cont.)

In 1998, the Joint Staff approved two **IW contingency plans** for CENTCOM combining both **electronic and physical attack**:

- **Operation FORCE FIELD**--a **theater-wide command and control warfare master plan** designed to provide "information dominance within a 500 km battle cube" and in particular render ineffective the key elements of a future regional opponent's **tactical** reconnaissance, air defense, and C3I systems.

- **Operation NET MASTER**--an **integrated regional strategic offensive IW plan** designed to cripple not only the adversary's military C3I and computer infrastructure but the **civilian** information infrastructure as well.

The Operation **NET MASTER** strategic IW plan would include:

- **Monitoring of the NII's of several specific countries** by an "IW cell" within the Pentagon with intelligence community support.

- **IW plans** for different components of specific target countries' energy, telecommunications, and information infrastructures **across a spectrum of damage levels** ranging from "temporary disruption to multi-month disablement."

- A special annex for **IW plans against the economic institutions** of specific countries (**including collateral damage assessments** for the regional and global economic system).

CENTCOM's IW planning also included **assessments of the vulnerability of key regional allies to IW effects** by potential adversaries.

SITUATION REPORT (cont.)

THE CRISIS

In Caracas

On **May 4, 2000, OPEC ministers met** in Caracas to review production and pricing policy. **Iran, Iraq, Libya, and Algeria were promoting a major cutback in production** with a goal of driving the price to "at least $60 (FY-95 dollars) a barrel."

The Caracas **OPEC meeting ended in total failure** and disarray after three days of tense discussions marked by a final televised **shouting match between the Iranian and Saudi oil ministers.**

In the Persian Gulf

On May 7 Iran announced that it would soon begin conducting **"military exercises appropriate to the evolving security situation in the Gulf."**

On May 8 the Saudi ruler called in the U.S. Ambassador and expressed **his deep concerns about the Iranians** whom he feared might use the OPEC stalemate as **an excuse for "a move of greatness" in the Gulf.**

On May 10, Tehran radio and television announced that the **Iranian Foreign Minister was flying to Riyadh with an "urgent proposal"** that would "resolve the OPEC stalemate" and "respond to the evolving security situation in the region."

On the evening of May 10, the U.S. Ambassador to Saudi Arabia reported on the contents of the Iranian "proposal:"

- **Iran, Iraq, Saudi Arabia and the other GCC states** should immediately **cut oil production by 20 percent**.

- The **GCC states** should **annul their military agreements with the U.S.** and declare "neutrality" or non-alignment.

- In return Iran would declare the GCC states to be under **"a new Iranian Persian Gulf security umbrella."**

The next day, May 11, U.S. intelligence detected the **preliminary mobilization of three of the six Iranian divisions located near Dezful in southwestern Iran,** including the mobilization of several regiments of heavy equipment transporters designed to rapidly move heavy armor and artillery.

At 2030 local time on May 11, **Saudi Arabia** ordered the **redeployment of one armored division** toward its border with Iraq and a **partial mobilization** of selected reserve elements. Two hours later **Kuwait** placed its army and reserves on a higher level of alert.

In Egypt

Later that night, **90% of the power in the Cairo area went out for several hours**.

In a message to the Secretary of State the U.S. Ambassador in Cairo noted that there was considerable **uncertainty** about whether the blackout was the product of **"deliberate sabotage or just Egyptian bad luck."**

In Washington

On the evening of May 11 the White House Situation Room received a message from the National Communications Center (NCC) indicating that **the public switched network for Northern California and Oregon had suffered a series of massive failures.**

The NCC also reported that, nearly simultaneously, the **base phone system in Fort Lewis, Washington had been subjected to a mass dialing attack** by personal computers--apparently orchestrated via the Internet--which paralyzed phone service for several hours.

On the PSN problem the NCC had "preliminary indications" that **a hidden "trap door" had apparently been placed into the latest release of code controlling the switching centers of the PSN.** The source of this problem was unclear although **a radical anti-interventionist group claimed responsibility** on the Internet.

In the Persian Gulf Region

At 0500 local time in the Gulf on May 12 (2200 EDT on the 11th), **two Saudi missile gunboats were fired upon by Iranian warships** discovered on an apparent intelligence collection mission off the coast of Al Jubayl.

SITUATION REPORT (cont.)

Twelve Saudi F-15s arrived on the scene in minutes and in the ensuing battle **both of the Saudi gunboats and three Iranian ships were sunk.** Minutes later fifteen Iranian MiG-29s and 31s arrived and in the air battle that followed **nine Iranian aircraft were downed at the cost of five Saudi F-15s.**

At 0630 local time on the 12th, **a S-3B *Viking*** from the CBG *Ronald Reagan* was **fired upon by an Iran missile frigate** while conducting a maritime surveillance mission **over the Straits of Hormuz.**

Thirty minutes later, **F/A-18s and F/A-14s from the *Reagan* found the frigate** some fifteen miles south of Bandar Abbas. The USN aircraft were **confronted by eight Iranian MiG-29s.** During the short air battle **three MiG-29s were shot down and the frigate was sunk** after receiving three *Harpoon* missile hits.

In Saudi Arabia

At 1100 local time on May 13, **the largest ARAMCO refinery near Dhahran had a catastrophic flow control malfunction** which led to a **large explosion and fire** at a brand new cracking tower.

This event was followed by a **"war communiqué" from a radical Islamic group linked to Iran** asserting that "the enemies of the true faith of Islam were vulnerable to the full range of Islamic might." The statement concluded with the **threat that the economy of the Saudi Kingdom "could be brought to its knees with the touch of a button."**

In a memcon to the Secretary of State, the U.S. Ambassador to Saudi Arabia warned that **the Saudi elite was "horrified by the prospect that Iran might have the capacity to severely disrupt their economy without firing a shot"** and beginning to express **concerns that the United States may be "unable to help the Saudi government respond to this new threat."**

In Moscow

At a news conference late on May 13 the Russian Foreign Minister called on the **UN Security Council to "immediately seek to mediate a settlement to the escalating crisis"** in the Persian Gulf.

In Tehran

At 0730 local time on May 14 (0030 EDT) **Iran** sent **messages to the GCC members, the U.S., the U.K., and France** calling for:

- A **cease-fire in place** of all forces on both sides.

- An **immediate freeze on further deployments by "foreign forces"** in the region.

- An **immediate summit at a neutral site** to discuss "a peaceful resolution of a crisis not of Iran's making."

The notes closed by stating that **"if there were not a positive response within 12 hours"** Iran would be **"forced to take actions consistent with its security rights and responsibilities in the Persian Gulf region."**

The notes to the leaders of Kuwait and Saudi Arabia also included a separate and explicit message that Iran would soon **"demonstrate the futility of depending upon the American imperialists for protection from modern weapons systems."**

Early that afternoon local time, **Iran fired three *Nodong I* MRBMs** virtually simultaneously from a field site south of Tehran. Two of the three successfully deployed **previously unseen exoatmospheric penetration aids**.

In Maryland

At 1812 EDT on May 14, the **new high-speed *Metro-Superliner* traveling at 300 km/hr slammed into an apparently mis-routed freight train** near Laurel, Maryland. Maryland State Police estimated that the train wreck had killed over 60 passengers and crew and critically injured another 120 persons.

Within three hours, the National Transportation Safety Board (NTSB) chief investigator notified the Secretary of Transportation that there was **"clear evidence" that the freight train had been misrouted onto the Metroliner track** with "some evidence" pointing to a sophisticated intrusion into the East Coast rail control system.

SITUATION REPORT (cont.)

In New York

At a mid-day reception on May 15 sponsored by the CPP, the **Iranian Ambassador** to the UN was overheard to state that **the United States** as "the technologically most advanced power on the planet" was **highly vulnerable to "21st Century attacks"** by **"states and others who had mastered contemporary computer and telecommunication technology."**

In Washington

Later on the 15th a preliminary report on the Metroliner crash by the DCI indicated that **a "logic bomb" had been placed into the Northeast rail computer systems, with "some tenuous evidence pointing to Iran."**

In passing the report to the President that evening the National Security Advisor noted that "NSA had **considerable doubts about the origin of the attack"** and questioned Iran's capacity to deploy "advanced polymorphic logic bombs." Further, he noted **that the FBI's Domestic Counter-terrorism Center was preparing a report voicing the strong suspicion that the tragedy was the product of a domestic conspiracy** which "may or may not be connected with the unfolding events in the Persian Gulf."

In the United Kingdom

At 1100 GMT on the 16th the Director of Scotland Yard informed the Prime Minister that **the Bank of England had detected "three different sniffer devices of new design in its main funds transfer system"** and that the Bank leadership was very fearful that unauthorized individuals could now enter the heretofore believed to be invulnerable funds transfer system.

In Atlanta and London

A few hours later CNN and ITN aired **"Special Report" stories** which featured the Metroliner train wreck in Maryland and leaked reports of problems with the Bank of England's funds transfer system. The CNN report stated that **"some Western intelligence agencies" believe that Iran may be employing computer experts from the Russian Mafiya** and "renegade software writers" from **India** to "threaten the entire economic fabric of the

United States and West Europe." The effect of both broadcasts was reinforced by interviews with a wide range of computer security experts.

The **London Stock Exchange Index fell 10% in late trading on the 16th** with investors shifting assets to safer havens.

In New York

At 1430 EDT on the 16th, **the New York Stock Exchange suffered its largest drop since the crash of 1987.** Even with the tripping of automatic exchange restraints, the Dow had fallen by nearly 200 points by the end of the day's trading. Analysts on CNBC and other business news networks speculated that major **institutional investors were attempting to get out** of the electronically managed market.

At 1500 the oil futures market closed with **the spot oil price at $75 a barrel. Gold prices for the day were up ten percent.**

At 1700 the Security and Exchange Commission(SEC)'s crisis investigating team informed the Secretary of Commerce that **"a pattern of institutional investment manipulation involving as yet unknown parties working through a set of European and Middle Eastern Banks"** had been **"a leading factor in the rapid acceleration in the Dow's mid-afternoon decline."**

In Washington

At noon EDT on May 17th the Consortium for Planetary Peace (CPP) announced that an **"emergency mobilization to stop an unnecessary and potentially devastating war"** would take place in the next 48 hours.

Two hours later the Consortium submitted a formal request to the U.S. Park Police for a permit for the Mall for May 21 for a **"demonstration of support for mediation and opposition to U.S. intervention in Saudi Arabia"** for **"an estimated 100,000 participants."** By nightfall similar permits had been requested in ten other major U.S. cities.

Approval of the Mall and other CPP requests seemed certain and **mobilization of CPP chapters began to** occur through **communiqués sent over the Internet and more traditional media outlets.**

SITUATION REPORT (cont.)

In the Persian Gulf

Early in the evening on the 18th after receiving reports on **further massing of Iranian armored forces for possible entry into southern Iraq**, increased Iranian naval activity near the Straits of Hormuz, and an Iranian "strategic alert," **USCINCCENT** sent a **message recommending the immediate execution of Phases I and II of the GREEN HORNET deployment plan for the Gulf.**

In Washington

An **emergency NSC meeting** was convened at 1500 EDT on the 18th to address USCINCCENT's recommendation and other military, diplomatic, and political issues related to the evolving Gulf crisis.

The meeting opened with an intelligence briefing by **the DCI** who noted that in terms of Iranian IW capability there was **"at this time no way of knowing for sure whether what we are seeing is:**

> **(1) Iranian testing of their strategic IW capability,**

> **(2) the beginning of an Iranian IW campaign to derail anticipated U.S. Gulf deployment plans, or**

> **(3) most of what we can expect from an Iranian strategic IW campaign."**

He also emphasized the added complication that **anti-interventionist domestic political groups** in both the U.S. and Europe **could be behind many of the IW incidents.**

The CJCS Chairman immediately emphasized that the **Time Phased Force Deployment List (TPFDL) for GREEN HORNET was very dependent on the ability to meet "a host of just-in-time logistic timelines" and would not tolerate "any significant disruption."**

In the highly speculative discussion that followed it was clear that in spite of "some circumstantial evidence" pointing to Iran **there remained considerable uncertainty about the extent of Iranian involvement in the recent IW incidents.**

After further reviewing the various issues on the table, the **President** announced the following **decisions**:

• Execution of **Phases I and II of GREEN HORNET.**

• Deployment of one-half all available CONUS-based **ATBM battalions to Egypt and Saudi Arabia.**

• Immediate convening of the **North Atlantic Council.**

• **Rejection** of any **diplomatic initiatives** at this time with: **(1) Iran or (2) the CIRD.**

• Congressional approval of his actions should be sought in **a resolution to be introduced in the Congress on the 19th.**

The President then indicated that he wanted the NSC to **"return later to give more time to IW issues."** He requested that **another full meeting of the NSC** take place **three hours hence** to **"make a set of IW decisions consistent with going forward with GREEN HORNET"** including dealing with "the deteriorating IW security situation at home."

The President admonished the NSC Advisor and the Press Secretary to **"keep the lid on very tight and downplay speculation"** regarding the extent of possible U.S. vulnerability to IW attacks and the origins of the attacks experienced to date.

He expressed particular concern that **decisions on the crisis could be made even more difficult** if there were public panic growing out of **"media hyping of the IW attack and attributing most of the actions to Iran when it might well be that much of the problem is coming from anti-interventionist forces in the United States."**

In Washington, London, and Paris

At 1630 EDT on the 18th at a **trilateral video conference** between the President, the British Prime Minister, and the President of France it was agreed that the U.K. and France would join in the U.S. response to the crisis and **execute SILVER SABRE.**

It was also agreed that the three countries should keep each other **fully informed of further developments in terms of possible IW attacks.**

STEP ONE: The Day Of...

INSTRUCTIONS

How to Proceed

1. You will have a total of roughly 50 minutes to complete your deliberations on STEP ONE.

2. Keep in mind that you are **in the role of a top advisor to the President** of the United States or to a National Security Council (NSC) principal in a group deliberative process akin to a classic time-urgent "pre-meeting" in advance of a formal NSC meeting with the President. The group's task is to revise a draft memo to the President in preparation for an NSC meeting scheduled for a few hours hence.

3. The Chair will lead a discussion that moves through the tasking described in the **Decisions to Be Made section to the right.** The Chair should ask one participant to record the group's recommendations.

4. It is suggested that the Chair begin by asking for participants in her/his group to <u>very briefly</u> (e.g., in a few sentences) give their **individual perspectives** on the basic challenge in the situation presented.

5. Keep in mind that the group is not being convened primarily as a decision-making body; **your principal responsibility is to craft a good issues and options memo** for the President. Nevertheless, as is always the case, the President will want to know if there is any group consensus on a preferred course of action on any issue.

6. The group's decisions (changes to the memo and recommendations where consensus can be achieved) should be **recorded** on the STEP ONE "Draft Memo for the President."

7. In noting the results of STEP ONE, the Chair of each group should keep in mind that she/he will be asked to **summarize very concisely** the group's deliberations and decisions on STEP ONE and STEP TWO at the end of STEP TWO.

Decisions to Be Made

I. Issues and Options

You are responding to a Presidential request to lay out the full range of issues and options that need to be addressed at the NSC meeting.

An NSC-led Working Group has been quickly convened and prepared the Draft Memo for the President on the following pages. It provides an initial cut at what might go forward to the President on a set of military, diplomatic, domestic, and declaratory policy issues.

Under the guidance of the Chair, the group should discuss this Draft Memo and expand and modify it as judged appropriate in the light of the situation.

In proceeding through the different sections of the Draft Memo (which can be taken up in a different order than that presented if the Chair so desires) the Chair should ascertain whether there are other critical issues beyond those presented on which Presidential decision-making is needed at this point in time--and modify the Draft Memo accordingly.

2. Recommendations

As the group settles on the individual issues and options to go forward to the President, the Chair should attempt to see **if consensus can be reached on recommendations** on individual issues--keeping in mind that at this point a consensus on all issues is not expected.

When it is clear to the Chair that there is a clear division of view on some issue, vote on the options still on the table and record the vote. In general, expect that on the most difficult and divisive issues the President will have to make the decisions in a traditional "The Buck Stops Here" capacity.

STEP ONE: The Day Of...

Draft Memo for the President of the United States

THE WHITE HOUSE

18 May 2000

MEMORANDUM FOR: The President of the United States

FROM: The National Security Advisor

SUBJECT: NSC Meeting on Persian Gulf Crisis - Information Warfare Issues

As you have requested, this NSC meeting will focus on the key information warfare (IW) issues that have emerged in the ongoing Persian Gulf crisis.

OBJECTIVES

Based on the discussion and decisions at the NSC Meeting earlier today, it would appear that the principal long-term objectives of the U.S. and its allies in this situation in terms of IW are:

• Demonstrate U.S. ability to detect, assess, and effectively defend against IW attacks.

• Deter future strategic IW attacks of the kind that we appear to be experiencing.

Our short-term objectives in terms of IW would appear to be:

• Enhance the prospects that the Saudi government will survive the combined threat (including the new IW elements) posed by the internal dissident movement and Persian regional ambitions.

• Reassure the American public that the National Information Infrastructure (NII) and transportation system is adequately protected against cyberspace threats.

MILITARY IW ISSUES

The tight timelines for both the GREEN HORNET and SILVER SABRE deployment plans raise concerns about the possible vulnerability of these plans to severe disruption by IW attack by either the Iranians or domestic political forces opposed to Western intervention in the Gulf crisis.

As this point we simply do not know the full extent of Iran's capacity to employ IW techniques to threaten critical elements of the U.S. NII and the NII's of our key allies and coalition partners. Nor do we know the extent of capabilities or intentions of those domestic forces which could seek to disrupt a U.S. deployment to the Gulf. (We may, in fact, only find some of the answers to such questions as we proceed with the execution of GREEN HORNET and SILVER SABRE.)

A key question at this time is whether we should take steps to help protect the NII and in particular the integrity of the Minimum Essential Information Infrastructure (MEII) for MRC contingencies.

You will also recall that GREEN HORNET has associated optional IW contingency plans that warrant consideration. These are:

> • FORCE FIELD, a battlefield IW plan and

> • NET MASTER, a strategic operation against a broad range of military and civilian infrastructure targets within Iran itself.

We may want to demonstrate in a selective fashion one or the other of these IW capabilities in order to further bolster the deterrent objective of the GREEN HORNET/SILVER SABRE deployments.

The military issues that need to be addressed at this meeting are thus:

1. What action, if any, should the U.S. take to enhance the prospects that the MEII will be able to support the timely deployment of forces associated with GREEN HORNET?

> _____ A. Take the following actions with respect to the MEII:

>> _____ Close all possible firewalls to the MEII to frustrate penetration and attack from within or outside the U.S..

>> _____ _____

>> _____ _____

>> _____ _____

_____ B. Take no action at this time.

2. What action, if any, should the United States take with respect to the FORCE FIELD and NET MASTER IW strike plans?

      _____ A. Deploy FORCE FIELD and NET MASTER assets into the Persian Gulf region.

      _____ B. Execute selected elements of FORCE FIELD and NET MASTER as a deterrent "warning shot" under the following caveats:

           _____ Only take actions which are surreptitious.

           _____ Only take actions which are non-lethal.

           _____ _____

      _____ C. Take no action at this time.

3. What emergency protective measures, if any, should we provide to the Saudis to assist them in defending their NII against further IW attack?

      _____ A. Provide the Saudis with dedicated secure communications equipment.

      _____ B. Assist the Saudis in taking control of selected PSN circuits.

      _____ C. _____

      _____ D. Provide no assistance of this character at this time.

4. _____

_____

      _____ A. _____

      _____ B. _____

DOMESTIC CYBERSPACE ISSUES

Although we do not want to alarm the American public about IW threats, we may need to take a set of defensive measures to increase the resilience of the NII-- and thus the domestic economy--against future IW attacks.

We could, for example, seek lower use rates in key distribution and transportation systems to better posture these systems with a surplus of capacity to respond to possible system disruptions caused by IW attacks on their information infrastructures. (In this context there will be no need to restrict utilization of the PSN as a whole since its vulnerability to disruption is not based upon capacity utilization but rather on the inherent flexibility of the network to reconstitute after an IW attack.)

You may also wish to consider ordering certain precautionary and contingency measures in the event there is further evidence of manipulation of institutional and other investor accounts in the stock market--and like problems in other key financial institutions. This could include the likes of financial and bank "holidays" to calm particular markets.

In considering the prospect that Iran may be attacking the U.S. through the use of American agents you may want to direct that there be some bridging of the traditional law enforcement-intelligence boundary to assess this prospect-- recognizing that this will require Congressional coordination and that public disclosure could prompt considerable controversy.

The following domestic cyberspace issue needs to be addressed:

1. Should actions be taken at this time to enhance protection of the NII against future attacks?

    _____ A. Yes. Take the following actions with respect to the NII:

        _____ Order all public power utilities and petroleum/gas pipeline companies to ask their users to prepare voluntary rationing plans to reduce system flow rates.

        _____ Restrict air traffic (general aviation) into key nodes to reduce air traffic control stress in the event of a major Air Traffic Control (ATC) system failure.

        _____ Direct CIA and NSA, in coordination with the FBI, to collect specific information about ties between domestic entities and foreign actors.

_____ _____

_____

_____ _____

_____

    _____ B. Not at this time.

2

The Day After...

...in Cyberspace

STEP TWO

RAND

3 June 1995

STEP TWO: The Day After...

SITUATION REPORT

THE CONTINUING CRISIS

In Washington

At the second May 18 NSC Meeting, the following actions were agreed:

- **Forward deployment** of assets associated with **FORCE FIELD and NET MASTER** but for now **no demonstrations** of capabilities.

- Providing **secure communications equipment to the Saudis.**

In addition the President decided that:

- The **MEII** should move to a **higher alert** level **"to insure execution of GREEN HORNET"** and **"close all possible electronic firewalls."**

- **Law enforcement agencies** should **not take any legal action against any U.S. organizations potentially collaborating with Iran or the CIRD at this time.**

- **No effort** should be made **to lower use rates in key energy distribution and transportation systems.**

In Washington

After a tempestuous debate which lasted until 1225 on May 20th, the Senate in the face of an aggressive lobbying campaign by the CPP, passed a resolution supporting the President's decision to send troops to the Persian Gulf. The margin of victory for the Administration was two votes.

In the Persian Gulf

On the morning of May 20th U.S. intelligence detected **the massing of a range of small high speed boats and landing craft several hundred kilometers north of the Iranian port of Bandar Abbas.** There was also clear evidence of a **build-up of helicopter and short take off and landing (STOL)** aircraft in several nearby airfields.

At the urging of USCINCCENT, **the Saudi government sent three brigades of National Guard units to King Khalid Military City**--a controversial decision because of **the prospect of further anti-government demonstrations in Riyadh and Dhahran.**

Intelligence reports indicate that **Iran has now mobilized all six of the armored and mechanized divisions around the Dezful area** in southwestern Iran.

In the United States

On the morning of May 20 DoD discovered that **the computer data base for the Time Phased Force Deployment List (TPFDL) had become plagued with "corrupt data."** The JCS IW planning cell's initial report on the problem indicated that **a computer worm--origin uncertain--had likely been unleashed inside the TPFDL software.**

In Atlanta

At 1210 EDT, May 20 the automatic tellers of the two largest bank chains in Georgia started to malfunction with bank clients being debited and/or credited thousands of the dollars after each ATM transaction--leading the banks in mid-afternoon to **shut down their ATM networks**.

Beginning at 1225 EDT, the **CNN news center feed out of Atlanta was intermittently off the air for a period of twelve minutes.**

Three hours later **a CNN "Special Report"** focused on **the vulnerability of the U.S. to "cyberspace warfare"**--dwelling on the Metroliner crash, the telephone outage in the Northwest, the ATM malfunctions in Atlanta, and the still-unexplained interference with CNN's own signal transmission. **Interviews accompanying the program conveyed a seeming growing sense of public concern** that the U.S. was **far more vulnerable to IW attack** than "the government has told us" in one angry interviewee's words.

SITUATION REPORT (cont.)

In the United States

Local and national evening news programs on May 20 reported that **U.S. military deployments to the Gulf were experiencing serious delays** due to **IW attacks on the local area networks and phone systems of a number of key Army and Marine bases.**

In Russia

At a Moscow news conference on the morning of May 21, the **Russian Foreign Minister criticized U.S. and allied deployments to the Gulf region as "dangerous brinkmanship"** but offered to host an international summit "to help defuse the increasingly dangerous crisis."

In Washington

The May 21 CPP **"anti-intervention" demonstration in Washington** far exceeded expectations with **a crowd estimated by the U.S. Park Police at over 400,000.** Many other well-attended demonstrations in both large and small cities across the country were also organized via the Internet.

In Cairo

On May 22 **the Egyptian government announced that it would "not send ground forces to Saudi Arabia at this point in time"** and called on Iran to "take steps to reduce the tension in the region."

A flash message from the U.S. Ambassador indicated that the President of Egypt was **"very concerned about Iran's capacity to cause economic and political damage in Egypt."**

In Chicago

At 1944 CST on May 22, the pilot of **a new Continental Airline's AB-340** making a final instrumented approach to **O'Hare International Airport** reported that his **flight deck avionics had suffered a massive malfunction** and that the aircraft was **"out of control and rolling over."**

At 2005, local police near O'Hare reported that **a large aircraft had crashed in a residential area south of the airport** "with no evidence of survivors." Within a half hour, local and Illinois State Police estimated that more than thirty persons had been killed on the ground with another 100 serious casualties.

In Washington

Three hours later--after receiving a preliminary British report concluding that **"all late model AB-340 and 330 flight control software may be infected by a sophisticated logic bomb"**--the Administrator of the FAA recommended that **all late model AB-340s and AB-330s "be immediately grounded"** until the precise nature of the flight deck malfunction could be ascertained and remedied.

At an NSC meeting later that day the Attorney General reported that FBI agents were **interrogating two suspects at a San Antonio, Texas software firm which had provided the most recent update of the AB-340 flight control software which had been made in response to the previously detected threat to the AirBus fight system integrity. Further, the Attorney General noted that the French Minister of the Interior via a video conference had identified the two suspects as clandestine members to the Texas chapters of the CIRD and the CPP.** Both suspects had recently received large cash payments through a Swiss bank **"from a foreign but unidentified source."**

The DCI then reported that two of the **Iranian heavy divisions engaged in supposed exercises were now approaching the Islamic Unity bridge south of Basra.** He also described a number of NSA intercepts suggesting that **the CIRD and allies within the Saudi military were preparing for "some type of major political action inside Saudi Arabia."**

SITUATION REPORT (cont.)

At this point **USCINCCENT** on a secure video hookup spoke up and voiced **"deep concern about remaining passive at this juncture."** He noted that "at any minute" **Iranian ground forces could** cross into Iraq or those Iranian naval, amphibious, and other units massing north of Bandar Abbas could move against Saudi Arabia. Should either situation emerge, he requested that he be given prior **authority to launch: (1) Operation IRON LANCE,** an all-out **preemptive air and missile strike against both Iranian force components** and (2) **major elements of FORCE FIELD.**

A highly contentious debate followed but no decision taken on USCINCCENT's request prior to the President having to leave for another meeting.

THE DAY AFTER

In Saudi Arabia

At 1920 local time (1220 EDT) on May 23, the news anchors of the two Saudi government TV networks were **suddenly replaced by the face of the head of the CIRD Council** who called on the citizens of Saudi Arabia **"to join forces in the peaceful transformation of the Saudi kingdom to freedom and democracy under Islam."**

This pre-arranged signal quickly led to **large scale demonstrations against the Saudi monarchy in Riyadh, Jiddah, Mecca, and Dhahran.**

At 1957 local time (1257 EDT) **the Saudi public switched network began to fail** apparently due to unauthorized **modification of the system through "trap doors" in the logic controlling its switches.**

U.S. experts assisting the Saudi government reported that the trap doors appeared to be **"very similar to those found earlier in the failure of the California-Oregon PSN."**

In Dhahran

At 2005 local time, the **local television station announced that the "Provisional Islamic Republic of Arabia" had now seized power in Dhahran and Mecca.**

Following this announcement, a self-described **"new military governor of Dhahran"** appeared and announced that "all Arabian citizens and members of the armed forces" should be prepared to **"welcome their Persian brothers who would soon arrive** to assist in the transformation to a new Islamic democracy in Saudi Arabia." He went on to state that **Iranian military assistance "would be immediately halted if foreign nations let the Arabian revolution proceed on its own."**

Ten minutes later **the commanding general of the U.S. 82nd Airborne Brigade**--on the ground at Dhahran international airfield with two battalions-- was ordered by CINCCENT to **refrain from any action other than to maintain control of the airfield** while he "sought guidance from Washington."

SITUATION REPORT (cont.)

In Riyadh

At 2130 local time in Riyadh **heavy fighting** broke out **between security police** near the King's Palace **and a column of National Guard motorized infantry which had pledged their loyalty to the new Provisional Islamic Republic.**

An hour later the U.S. Ambassador reported that fighting was spreading rapidly throughout the city and that **"a coup attempt was underway with the location of the King unknown."**

In Washington

At 1610 local time in Washington the Secretary of Defense was informed by the CJCS that **"a full-scale IW attack by unknown sources"** was underway at **"almost every military base in the United States and Europe involved in GREEN HORNET and SILVER SABRE"**--with deep concern as to whether the MEII here and in Europe "can withstand the ongoing assault."

The CJCS expressed "the hope" that a **preliminary assessment of the impact** of this IW campaign would be **available within a few hours** "though it could be much longer."

He also **described the TPFDL as "a goddamned mess"** and said that the Joint Staff was "frantically trying to patch together a new deployment plan." He admitted, however, that he **"had no idea just what kind of GREEN HORNET schedule was now achievable."**

In the Persian Gulf Region

At 2300 local time in the Gulf (1700 EDT), **USCINCCENT** cabled that **"the movement of Iranian forces across the Gulf toward Dhahran appeared to be imminent."**

In Atlanta

At a news conference held at the CNN news room, the members of the **"Executive Council" of the Consortium for Planetary Peace** denounced the "criminal action which led to the AirBus tragedy at O'Hare." but concluded that "legitimate protest should not be quashed by

the terrorist acts of a few" by announcing that the CPP was **"mobilizing all of its chapters to conduct civil disobedience actions** to stop the U.S. Government's mad dash to war to save an undemocratic and failed Saudi regime."

In the Persian Gulf

At 0200 local time on May 24 USCINCCENT reported to the CJCS that **"several JSTARS aircraft operating in the Gulf region appeared to be plagued with a computer worm triggered by some external source."**

At 0600 CINCCENT reported that **Saudi loyalists had regained control of Mecca and most of the city Riyadh.** Military units supporting the Provisional Islamic Republic and their supporters had at this point **withdrawn to the northern suburbs "but probably only temporarily."**

In Savannah, Georgia

The **Coast Guard and local police at Savannah harbor had to use fire hoses to break-up a flotilla of sailing and power boats which were attempting to "blockade" the sealift ship USS Bob Hope** from sailing to the Persian Gulf. Similar **incidents occurred in Galveston and San Diego harbors**.

In Riyadh

At 0700 local time on the 24th the U.S. Ambassador sent a message reporting that **the King and his entourage are voicing confidence that "trends were in their favor"** for regaining control of the domestic situation inside Saudi Arabia but **"immediate and decisive American, British, and French action" would be key to suppressing disloyal army units** and **"keeping the Persians off the Arabian peninsula."**

The Ambassador noted that the situation inside Saudi Arabia appeared to him to be **"much more dicey"** than the King and his entourage were **prepared to admit.**

SITUATION REPORT (cont.)

Dover, Delaware

At 0630 EST on May 24, **the driver of cement truck was shot dead by USAF police during an attempt crash the main gate at Dover Air Force Base.** Latter reports to the Secretary of Defense from the USAF Chief of Staff indicated that the **incident was part of a larger plan described on the Internet by the "action arm" of the CPP to block the runways to any further use by the C-5 fleet home-based at Dover.**

In Washington

At 1030 EST on May 24, the **entire phone network in the Washington/Baltimore region including local cellular systems failed.** A preliminary assessment suggested **an attack through trap doors** not unlike those which caused the earlier PSN failure in the Northwest.

In Chicago

At 1330 EDT, **the Chicago Commodity Exchange experienced some of its "wildest fluctuations in history".** Amongst many knowledgeable traders and the leadership of the Exchange, there was **widespread suspicion that "the Exchange was being subjected to a powerful form of electronic manipulation by parties unknown."**

In London

At the close of the spot oil market **on May 24 the price for crude oil topped $100 a barrel.**

In New York

The value of the dollar fell by 5 percent versus the Yen, Mark, and Peso while the London and New York Stock Exchanges fluctuated widely **with both closing down by three percent**.

In Washington

An emergency NSC meeting was arranged in the late afternoon on the 24th with great difficulty because of the phone shutdown. The JCS Chairman "regrettably acknowledged" that **the IW campaign in both the U.S. and Europe and in Saudi Arabia had been "remarkably successful"** and that **"further efforts to inhibit GREEN HORNET and SILVER SABRE by domestic sources as well as Iran were expected."**

He painted a **very gloomy picture** of a probable **very slow buildup** of U.S. and allied forces in the region with **"little or no cooperation"** from previously assumed stalwart coalition partners like Egypt and Turkey followed by **"a difficult multi-month campaign** to thwart any immediate Iranian move across the Gulf toward Dhahran while deterring a likely follow-on Iranian invasion of Kuwait and northern Saudi Arabia through Iraq."

The DCI observed that a "probably reliable" **HUMINT source** in Baghdad is reporting that **Iraq has given permission to Iran to move forces across the Islamic Unity Bridge south of Basra.**

The Secretary of State noted that the **Saudi government** had apparently **"lost confidence in the ability of the U.S and its allies to defend the country under current circumstances."** He emphasized that all of these factors **"would provide domestic opponents with a field day in politically opposing aggressive U.S. action in the region."**

USCINCCENT noted that it was "still early in the day" and reiterated his request for authority to launch **air operations against Iran if any of its forces move across the Gulf or across the Islamic Unity Bridge into Iraq.**

The Secretary of the Treasury reminded the members of the NSC, "that the President faced a major domestic crisis with multiple dimensions which included great turmoil in the currency, stock, and commodities markets." To emphasize his point, he stated that the Secret Service had monitored a "torrent of vitriol and abuse aimed at the Administration and person of the President on the Internet."

The Attorney General added that there had been "an explosion of anti-Islamic incidents throughout the United States including the firebombing of the offices of the CIRD in Chicago, Houston, and Los Angeles."

SITUATION REPORT (cont.)

The President halted the NSC meeting in order to **take an urgent call from the Russian President** on the Hotline regarding his proposed **cease-fire resolution in the UN Security Council and offer to personally mediate the Gulf crisis.** The President requested that the meeting be resumed in two hours and that a brief issues and options paper "that faces squarely the IW threat to our strategy in the Gulf" be prepared for his consideration at that time.

In New York

At 0630 EDT, May 24, CBS Evening News was interrupted for seven minutes by the "Action Arm of the Committee for Planetary Peace". During the video take-over, the CPP spokesperson, a well known and highly regarded media personality, called for wide-spread civil disobedience to thwart an Administration which had, "lost touch with domestic and international reality."

In measured tones, the spokesperson noted that Congress had been deceived into giving a *carte blanche* to an Executive "bent on war" during the Gulf of Tonkin resolution in 1965. **The spokesperson concluded that it was the duty of all citizens to "oppose by all possible peaceful means this government which was intent on dragging the United States into an unwanted and unneeded war ."**

STEP TWO: The Day After...

INSTRUCTIONS

How to Proceed

1. You will have a total of 50 minutes for STEP TWO--roughly 10 minutes for reading and 40 minutes for deliberations.

2. Your instructions are the same as in STEP ONE. The group's task is again to revise a draft memo to the President in preparation for an imminent NSC meeting.

3. It is again recommended that the Chair begin by soliciting the group for individual perspectives on the situation presented.

4. The Chair of the group should keep in mind that she/he will be asked to devote approximately two minutes to a summary of the group's Step Two deliberations and decisions as part of the summary reporting out (of STEP ONE and STEP TWO) at the end of STEP TWO.

Decisions to Be Made

I. Issues and Options

You are responding to a Presidential request to lay out the political-military issues and options that need to be addressed at the NSC meeting in roughly an hour.

The NSC staff has prepared the Draft Memo for the President provided on the following pages. It constitutes an initial cut at what might go forward to the President in this situation.

2. Recommendations

Keep in mind that the group is not being convened primarily as a decision-making body. **Your principal responsibility is to craft a good issues and options memo for the President.**

However, under the leadership of the Chair **the group should make an attempt to achieve consensus recommendations** on the principal issues in the Draft Memo--keeping in mind that the achievement of **such consensus will be appreciated and valued by the President, but not necessarily expected**.

Again when it is clear to the Chair that there is a division of view, vote on the options still on the table and record the vote.

STEP TWO: The Day After...

Draft Memo for the President

The White House

24 May 2000

MEMORANDUM FOR: The President

FROM: The National Security Advisor

SUBJECT: The Crisis in Saudi Arabia and Related Information
Warfare Issues

As requested this memorandum lays out the key issues for consideration at
the 8:00 pm NSC Meeting on the crisis in Saudi Arabia.

OBJECTIVES

We would appear to have the following explicit near-term objectives in this
context:

• To take whatever measures are necessary to forestall the collapse of
the legitimate government of Saudi Arabia (including reassuring the
Saudis that disruptive IW actions will not significantly affect our ability
to meet our security commitments in the Gulf).

• To demonstrate clearly to the global community that the use of
emerging strategic IW techniques does not constitute a legitimate means
of effecting political change in any nation.

• To reassure the American and allied publics that threats to the security
of their National Information Infrastructures and transportation
systems can be effectively contained.

MILITARY AND STRATEGY ISSUES

A fundamental decision at this point in the crisis is whether we should seek
to de-escalate this conflict (taking advantage of the Russian offer to work
this problem in the UN Security Council) or continue to move forces into the
region and take other actions on a timetable which recognizes the challenge
of overcoming continuing Iranian, CIRD, and possibly domestic IW efforts.

There is also the question of whether the United States should reply with the offensive use of IW techniques to demonstrate to Iran--and globally--that the United States has a powerful retaliation option other than the force of arms. (An important question here is our ability to assess collateral damage if we launch an aggressive IW attack on the Iranian economic infrastructure.)

The regional strategic offensive IW plan currently on the table--NET MASTER--targets different components of Iran's military C3I, and its energy, telecommunications, information, and other infrastructures across a spectrum of damage levels ranging from "temporary disruption to multi-month disablement." We might demonstrate this offensive IW capability in some fashion (keeping in mind the uncertainty of whether the Iranians will see and interpret that demonstration as we wish) or proceed with the full attack plan against selected targets sets.

The military and strategy issues that must be addressed are as follows:

1. Should we pursue a de-escalation strategy based on accepting the cease-fire and mediation proposal by Moscow?

    _____ A. Not at this time

    _____ B. Yes, but with conditions:

        • _____

        • _____

2. What form should our IW response take?

    _____ A. Demonstration of IW capability.

    _____ B. Execute major elements of NET MASTER.

3. If we launch an IW response against Iran the targets and objectives (set back of weeks, months, etc. to recovery) of those IW strikes would be:

    _____ Energy infrastructure (set back _____).

    _____ Telecommunications infrastructure (set back _____).

    _____ Oil/Petroleum infrastructure (set back _____).

    _____ Banking system (set back _____).

    _____ Transportation system (set back _____).

    _____ _____

    _____ _____

4. _____

_____

_____ A. _____

_____ B. _____

DIPLOMATIC ISSUES

We need to organize as powerful a collective response as possible in this difficult situation which probably means in part working through the UN Security Council. In addition to preparing a coordinated response with the United Kingdom and France, we must prepare nations like the Russian Federation and China for the prospect that our military response to this crisis might lead to full-scale war in the region.

We also need to revisit the question of whether to undertake any direct contacts with Iran or the CIRD.

The diplomatic issues to be considered now are:

1. If we decide accept Moscow's cease-fire and mediation proposal, should we seek a formal meeting of the U.N. Security Council?

_____ A. Yes and try to gain support from the PRC.

_____ B. Not at this time.

2. Should we contact Britain and France and raise the prospect of contacting the CIRD with the objective of negotiating a peaceful transition to a more democratic government in Saudi Arabia?

_____ A. Yes

_____ B. Not at this time

3. _____

_____

_____ A. _____

_____ B. _____

DOMESTIC CYBERSPACE ISSUES

You will recall from the NSC Meeting on May 18 that elements of the US economic infrastructure which rely heavily on the efficient use of the NII might take defensive measures to reduce their overall vulnerability to IW type attacks. You will also recall that there is an issue as to how to respond to the prospect that Iran may be attacking the U.S. through the use of American agents. You decided at the May 18th NSC meeting that you would not initiate coordinated action by the intelligence community and the FBI, to collect specific information about ties between domestic entities and foreign actors. In light of recent events that issue would appear to warrant being revisited.

The following domestic cyberspace issues need to be addressed:

1. Should we declare a series of financial and bank "holidays" to calm the troubled financial, stock, and commodity markets?

_____ A. Yes, the following markets should closed for 48 hours:

_____ The three national stock exchanges

_____ The Chicago and New York commodity exchanges

_____ The Interstate Banks

_____ B. Not at this time

2. What other actions should be taken at this time to enhance protection of the NII against future attacks?

_____ A. Take the following actions with respect to the NII:

_____ Order all public power utilities and petroleum/gas pipeline companies to ask their users to prepare voluntary rationing plans to reduce system flow rates.

_____ Restrict air traffic (general aviation) into key nodes to reduce air traffic control stress in the event of a major Air Traffic Control (ATC) system failure.

_____ Direct CIA and NSA, in coordination with the FBI, to collect specific information about ties between domestic entities and foreign actors.

_____ _____

_____ _____

_____ B. Take no additional actions at this time.

3

The Day After...

...in Cyberspace

STEP THREE

RAND

3 June 1995

STEP THREE: The Day Before...

INSTRUCTIONS

How to Proceed

1. You will have a total of approximately 45 minutes for your reading and deliberations on STEP THREE.

2. The time period is the very near future--say the fall of this year.

3. You are again in the role of a top advisor to the President or an NSC principal and a participant in a high-level interagency meeting preparing for a later NSC meeting with the President.

4. You will be given roughly five minutes to quickly review the STEP THREE Draft Memo for the President.

5. The Chair will then lead a discussion that moves through the tasking described in the Decisions to Be Made section to the right--which follows essentially the same basic process as the previous two steps.

Decisions to Be Made

I. Issues and Options

The objective of this NSC meeting is to obtain the President's decisions on a set of near-term issues that have emerged from a study commissioned by a Presidential Review Directive on: (1) threats to national security and safety arising from the evolution of new information warfare (IW) techniques and (2) strategies that can be used to help counter those threats.

The NSC staff-prepared Draft Memo for the President (on the pages immediately following) is designed to serve this purpose.

Under the guidance of the Chair, the group should discuss this Draft Memo and expand and modify it as judged appropriate.

2. Recommendations

When the group settles on the material to go forward to the President, it should attempt under the Chair's leadership to **see if it can reach consensus** on a recommendation on the issues in the Draft Memo - keeping in mind that **consensus is not necessarily expected;** the President invariably will have to make some decisions.

When it is clear to the Chair that there is a division of views on an issue, vote on the options still on the table and record the vote.

STEP THREE: The Day Before...

Draft Memo for the President

The White House

xx October 1995

MEMORANDUM FOR: The President

FROM: The National Security Advisor

SUBJECT: Threats to National Security and Safety from the New Techniques of Information Warfare

There will be a National Security Council meeting tomorrow on threats to national security and safety arising from the evolution of new information warfare (IW) techniques, and possible steps that might be taken at this time to respond to those threats.

A recent interagency study of this subject has confirmed that our "national interests" are increasingly dependent on a set of information systems critical not only to U.S. military command, control, and intelligence capability, but also more broadly to U.S. health, safety, and commerce. This set of vital information systems appears to be vulnerable to a spectrum of IW attacks, including disruption and denial of service, implanting false data, covert installation of harmful programs (e.g., viruses), and the outright theft of information. Unlike other threats to U.S. national security, the "cost of entry" to potential attackers is extremely low, enabling attacks to be initiated by other nations, "hackers", terrorists, zealots, disgruntled insiders, criminals, and commercial organizations.

Because of the unconventional nature of this new strategic threat, it is increasingly clear that traditional roles and missions of agencies within the federal government are not fully appropriate to assessing risks and devising counters to specific threats.

Another problem is that "Cyberspace" transcends our national borders and has traditionally been a forum exhibiting and facilitating freedom of interconnection and expression. There are no current regulations or licensing provisions governing who can connect to the Internet, much less government-mandated systems and security provisions. This raises questions as to how aggressive the U.S. can or should be in pursuing the imposition of restrictions on cyberspace.

The set of strategy and policy issues set forth below attempt to give structure and clarity to several key facets of this complex problem that would appear to warrant near-term attention.

UNDERSTANDING CYBERSPACE RISKS

In a new and dynamic strategic arena like cyberspace all elements of threat, vulnerability, and risk assessment--and warning--present daunting problems. The problems that follow present particularly difficult challenges.

1. <u>IW Risk Assessment</u>. Should a formal IW risk assessment organization be established to: (1) assess U.S. vulnerabilities and associated risks and (2) conduct routine net assessments of evolving IW threats?

_____ A. Yes. Establish such an organization; assign the responsibility of executive agent to:

_____ The Secretary of Defense.

_____ The Secretary of Commerce.

_____ The Attorney General

_____ The Director of Central Intelligence.

_____ The Director of the National Security Agency.

_____ The Director of the Federal Emergency Management Agency (FEMA)

_____ The National Communications System (NCS)/The National Security Telecommunications Advisory Committee (NSTAC)

_____ A new independent federal agency.

_____ B. Not at this time.

2. <u>IW Strategic/Tactical Warning and Attack Assessment</u>. Should a formal strategic and tactical warning and attack assessment coordinating function be assigned to some government entity?

_____ A. Yes. Give the responsibility to:

_____ The National Security Agency.

_____ The Central Intelligence Agency.

_____ The National Communication System/NSTAC.

_____ The Domestic Terrorism Center

_____ A new independent agency such as that cited above.

_____ _____

_____ B. Not at this time.

IDENTIFYING CYBERSPACE RISK MITIGATION MEASURES

What steps can and should be taken to meet the critical needs of cyberspace safety and security while retaining to the degree possible the broad benefits of the open information architecture and information-sharing that has to date characterized the National Information Infrastructure (NII) and the Global Information Infrastructure (GII)?

In this context a key issue for near-term decision is whether to launch an effort to establish a Minimum Essential Information Infrastructure (MEII) to meet a variety of national security emergency preparedness needs--for example, insuring that regional force deployments that depend heavily on the operations of segments of the NII are resilient to attack.

1. Minimum Essential Information Infrastructure. Should the United States develop an Minimum Essential Information Infrastructure to assure the survivability and effectiveness under adverse conditions of key military-related systems within the NII (and possibly also the GII)?

_____ A. Yes; for day-to-day use (i.e., no warning dependence).

_____ B. Yes; for emergency use only (i.e., warning dependent transitions acceptable).

_____ C. No; it is not necessary at this time.

_____ D. No; it is not feasible because key NII infrastructure components are too interdependent to isolate a manageable subset as "minimum essential."

_____ E. _____

2. If we decide that an MEII of some kind needs to be developed , who should be given the responsibility for organizing the process (e.g. a "Network Security Steering Committee") that chooses the initial elements of the NII to be included in the MEII?

_____ A. The National Security Council.

_____ B. The White House Domestic Policy Staff.

_____ C. The Office of Science and Technology Policy (OSTP).

_____ D. The Department of Defense (DoD).

_____ E. The Department of Commerce.

_____ F. The National Communication System/NSTAC.

_____ G. A new independent federal IW agency.

_____ _____

NEAR-TERM POLICY COORDINATION

How should the executive branch handle the near-term coordination of IW-related activities and related communications with industry and other extra-governmental entities?

1. <u>An Administration Focal Point</u>. Should a senior administration policy official be designated as the focal point for coordinating <u>near-term</u> executive branch activity on cyberspace defense?

    _____ A. Yes. Give the responsibility to a senior official:

        _____ On the National Security Council Staff.

        _____ On the White House Domestic Policy Staff.

        _____ In OSTP.

        _____ In DoD.

        _____ In Commerce.

        _____ In the Office of Management and Budget.

        _____ In FEMA.

        _____ _____

    _____ B. Not at this time.